MO TZU

*Prepared for the Columbia College Program of
Translations from the Asian Classics*
WM. THEODORE DE BARY, *Editor*

MO TZU

 BASIC WRITINGS

Translated by BURTON WATSON

New York and London

COLUMBIA UNIVERSITY PRESS

Preparation of this work was done under a grant from the Carnegie Corporation of New York to the Committee on Asian Studies for the production of texts to be used in undergraduate education. That Corporation is not, however, the author, owner, publisher, or proprietor of this publication, and is not to be understood as approving by virtue of its grant any of the statements made or views expressed.

FOREWORD

Mo Tzu: Basic Writings is one of a group of publications, the Translations from the Asian Classics, through which the Committee on Asian Studies has sought to transmit to Western readers representative works of the Asian traditions in thought and literature. In its volumes of source readings forming the "Introduction to Asian Civilizations," the Committee has provided a broad selection of excerpts from influential thinkers in India, China, and Japan, discussing the great problems of their times. Excerpts from Mo Tzu are thus included in *Sources of Chinese Tradition.* Several of the great philosophers of classical China, however, deserve a fuller reading and analysis than such a survey allows, and there has been a need for more complete translations of them. To say this is not to deprecate the excellent work already done by pioneer scholars in opening these writers up to the West. Often, however, their translations have not been kept in print or available at prices most readers could afford. To give them much wider circulation in the home and classroom than heretofore is the aim of this series.

We are indebted to Professor Watson that he has been willing to devote his considerable talents and learning to meet this need for accurate translations of basic works. No doubt it would have been personally more gratifying to the researcher's instinct in him, and in the professional fraternity, had he turned to some untouched subject, no

matter how obscure and out-of-the-way. That he has returned to several of the old masters is a credit both to
them and to him. Great figures like Mo Tzu, Hsün Tzu,
and Han Fei Tzu—and let us hope Chuang Tzu will join
them in this series—merit rediscovery and reexamination
by each generation. How much more is this true when,
in comparison to Confucius and Lao Tzu, they have been
known until now by so few!

WM. THEODORE DE BARY

CONTENTS

OUTLINE OF EARLY CHINESE HISTORY

(Dates and entries before 841 B.C. are traditional)

B.C.	Dynasty	
2852		Fu Hsi, inventor of writing, fishing, trapping.
2737	Culture Heroes	Shen Nung, inventor of agriculture, commerce.
2697		Yellow Emperor.
2357		Yao.
2255	Sage Kings	Shun.
2205		Yü, virtuous founder of dynasty.
1818	Hsia Dynasty	Chieh, degenerate terminator of dynasty.
1766	Shang or Yin Dynasty	King T'ang, virtuous founder of dynasty.
[c. 1300]		[Beginning of archeological evidence.]
1154		Chou, degenerate terminator of dynasty.

Dynasty	Date (B.C.)	Event
Three Dynasties		
	1122	King Wen, virtuous founder of dynasty.
	1115	King Wu, virtuous founder of dynasty.
Chou Dynasty — Western Chou		King Ch'eng, virtuous founder of dynasty.
		(Duke of Chou, regent to King Ch'eng)
	878	King Li.
	781	King Yu.
	771	
	722	Spring and Autumn period (722–481).
Eastern Chou	551	Period of the "hundred philosophers" (551–c. 233): Confucius, Mo Tzu, Lao Tzu (?), Mencius, Chuang Tzu, Hui Shih, Shang Yang, Kung-sun Lung, Hsün Tzu, Han Fei Tzu.
	403	Warring States period (403–221).
	4th to 3d cent.	Extensive wall-building and waterworks by Ch'in and other states.
	249	Lü Pu-wei, prime minister of Ch'in.
Ch'in Dynasty (221–207 B.C.)	221	The First Emperor; Li Ssu, prime minister.
	214	The Great Wall completed.

MO TZU

 *INTRODUCTION*

Almost nothing is known about the life of Mo Ti, or Master Mo, the founder of the Mo-ist school of philosophy. A number of anecdotes in which he figures are found in the *Mo Tzu,* the book compiled by his disciples to preserve the teachings of their master, and other late Chou and early Han works contain scattered references to him and his school. But they tell us little about the man himself. He seems to have lived some time between the death of Confucius in 479 B.C. and the birth of Mencius in 372 B.C., flourishing probably in the latter half of the fifth century B.C. He is identified by some writers as a native of the state of Sung, by others as a native of Lu, the birthplace of Confucius. The *Huai-nan Tzu* (ch. 21), a work of the second century B.C., says that he first studied under the scholars of the Confucian school (though in later years he bitterly attacked the Confucians), and certainly the frequency with which he quotes from the *Book of Odes* and the *Book of Documents* would seem to indicate that at some point he received thorough instruction in these ancient texts. Like Confucius and Mencius, he apparently traveled a good deal, visiting one after another of the feudal rulers of the time in an attempt to gain a hearing for his ideas, and we are told that for a while he served as a high minister in the state of Sung. He was particularly anxious to spread his doctrine of universal love and to persuade the rulers of his day to cease their incessant attacks upon each other. The *Mo Tzu* (sec. 50), for example, relates that, when he heard that Ch'u was planning an attack on Sung, he walked for ten days and ten nights to reach the court of Ch'u, where he succeeded in persuading the ruler to call off the expedition.

Mo Tzu and his followers believed that such attacks could be stopped not only by preaching sermons on universal love, but by strengthening the defenses of vulnerable states so as to diminish the chances of a profitable victory for aggressors. Thus they hastened to the aid of besieged states, and in time became experts on methods of warfare. They formed close-knit, disciplined bands (the school was said to have split into three groups after Mo Tzu's death), headed by an "elder" whose word was law and who, when death drew near, selected his successor from among the group. Later followers of the school also took up the study of logic, though perhaps, as Arthur Waley has suggested, this was less from any intrinsic interest in the subject than from a desire "to arm themselves against modernist attack." [1]

The *Mo Tzu*, a work in fifteen chapters and seventy-one sections, of which eighteen are now lost, reflects these interests of the later Mo-ist school, containing a number of sections on logic and military science. Of more importance in the history of Chinese thought, however, are the sections which expound the political and ethical ideas of Mo Tzu himself, and it is from these sections that the excerpts translated here have been selected.

The sections chosen deal with eleven topics, each topic being stated in the title of the section. Each section is divided into three subsections except the last, that entitled "Against Confucians," which is divided into two. Over the centuries, however, some of these subsections have been lost, so that only six of the eleven sections are complete today. The subsections

[1] Arthur Waley, *The Way and Its Power* (London, Allen and Unwin, 1934), p. 65.

within each section often differ in wording, order of ideas, and even slightly in content. But on the whole they resemble each other so closely that they appear to be no more than slightly different versions of a single lecture or sermon. As stated above, the Mo-ist school was said to have split into three groups after the death of its founder, and scholars have surmised that the three treatments of each topic may represent the doctrines of Mo Tzu as they were handed down in each of the three groups. In the translation I have, in order to avoid repetition, in most cases translated only the subsection which seemed to contain the most interesting and complete exposition of each topic, though in a few cases I have translated two subsections dealing with a single topic. All but the last section contain frequent uses of the formula "Master Mo Tzu said," which would seem to indicate that they were written down not by Mo Tzu himself but by his disciples, though it is not altogether impossible that Mo Tzu wrote some of them himself, and that the phrase was added later by redactors.

Before discussing the specific doctrines expounded in the portion of the work presented here, I wish to say a word about Mo Tzu's method of argumentation. In the section entitled "Against Fatalism," Mo Tzu lists three "tests" or criteria which are to be used to determine the validity of any theory: 1) its origin, by which he means whether or not it conforms with what we know of the practices of the sage kings of antiquity; 2) its validity, i.e., whether or not it conforms with what we know from the evidence of the senses; 3) its applicability, i.e., whether, when put into practice, it will bring benefit to the state and the people. Though Mo Tzu does not always employ all three in each case, these are the principal criteria upon which he bases his arguments.

The modern reader will probably experience the greatest

difficulty in accepting the pertinence of Mo Tzu's first criterion. All of us today tend to be skeptical of "what history
proves," since we have seen history cited to prove so many
disparate and even contradictory assertions. Moreover the "history" which Mo Tzu cites to prove his arguments is often,
even to the eye of the nonspecialist, patently no more than
legend and myth. We must remember, however, that in Mo
Tzu's day, so far as we can gather, the majority of educated
Chinese accepted without question the following two assumptions: 1) that, at certain periods in the past, enlightened rulers
had appeared in China to order the nation and raise Chinese
society to a level of peace, prosperity, and moral vigor un-
paralleled in later days; 2) that, in spite of the paucity of
reliable accounts, it was still possible to discover, mainly
through the records contained in the *Book of Odes* and *Book
of Documents,* how these rulers had acted and why—that is,
to determine "the way of the ancient sage kings"—and to
attempt to put it into practice in the present age. The appeal
to the example of antiquity, which Mo Tzu so often uses to
clinch his argument, therefore carried enormous weight in his
day, and continued to do so in Chinese philosophy down to
the present century. By making such an appeal, he was following the approved practice of the thinkers of his age, and we
may suppose that, if his listeners accepted the validity of his
account of antiquity, they must have felt strongly compelled
to accept his conclusions.

The second criterion, the appeal to the evidence of the
senses, he uses much less frequently, and then often with
disastrous results, as when he argues for the existence of ghosts
and spirits on the basis of the fact that so many people have
reportedly seen and heard them.

His third criterion, that of practicability, needs no comment, since it is as vital a part of argumentative writing today as it was in Mo Tzu's time.

The eleven sections representing the basic doctrines of Mo Tzu are entitled: "Honoring the Worthy," "Identifying with One's Superior," "Universal Love," "Against Offensive Warfare," "Moderation in Expenditures," "Moderation in Funerals," "The Will of Heaven," "Explaining Ghosts," "Against Music," "Against Fatalism," and "Against Confucians."

As will be noticed, Mo Tzu was "agin" quite a number of things, and this fact provides a valuable clue to his personality and the character of his thought. He seems to have been a passionately sincere but rather dour and unimaginative man who, observing the social and moral ills of his time and the suffering which they brought to so many of the common people, felt personally called upon to attempt a cure. One way of accomplishing his aim, he believed, was to attack the abuses of the feudal aristocrats and literati. So deep is his compassion for the common people, and so outspoken his criticisms of their rulers, that some scholars have recently been led to speculate that Mo, which means "tattoo," may not be a surname at all, but an appellation indicating that Master Mo was an ex-convict who had undergone the punishment of being tattooed, and flouted the fact in the face of society by adopting the name of his penalty. This suggestion, interesting as it is, seems highly dubious, for, no matter how great his compassion for the common people may have been, his teachings were meant primarily for the ears of the rulers, and if he hoped to gain a hearing among them he would hardly have proclaimed himself a breaker of their laws. If Mo is not a surname, it is probably an appellation adopted by Mo Tzu, or given to him by his contemporaries, the meaning of which is now lost.

It is true, however, that Mo Tzu and his followers seem to have taken a far sterner and less compromising attitude toward the ruling class of the time and its foibles than did the members of the other philosophical schools. The Mo-ists condemned the music, dances, and luxurious living of the aristocracy because such pastimes taxed the wealth and energy of the common people and added nothing to the material welfare of the nation. (They failed to note the benefit which such pastimes provided for the class of merchants, artisans, entertainers, and servants who catered to such tastes, since for the Mo-ists, as for almost all early Chinese thinkers, the only common people who deserved consideration were the farmers.) They denounced offensive warfare for the same reasons, because it was a burden and an expense to the people and provided little in the way of material benefit, and they likewise condemned elaborate funerals and all other "unnecessary" expenditures. They attacked fatalistic thinking because they wanted men to believe that wealth and good fortune came only in response to virtuous deeds, and opposed the Confucian scholars because Confucianism taught such fatalistic doctrines and encouraged music and elaborate funeral rites.

Such is the negative side of Mo Tzu's thought, a listing of the ideas and practices which he believed must be abandoned before society could be restored to peace and order. On the positive side, the first principle which he enunciates is that called "honoring the worthy"—the duty of rulers to seek out men of wisdom and virtue and employ them in their governments. This would seem to be a reasonable and innocuous enough doctrine. By Mo Tzu's time, the right of certain aristocratic families to maintain hereditary possession of ministerial posts in the feudal governments had already been seriously challenged, and many rulers were doing just what Mo

Tzu recommended—surrounding themselves with men chosen from the lower aristocracy or the common people who would be less encumbered by family ties and feel a greater personal devotion to the ruler who had promoted them. And no other philosophical school could be expected to take exception to Mo Tzu's doctrine, since each would no doubt interpret "worthy men" to mean "our party"—except perhaps the Taoists and farmer-recluses, who professed not to be interested in acquiring government posts anyway. Mo Tzu may have been among the first to give clear and unequivocal expression to this ideal, which became a commonplace in Chinese political thought. But the growing conviction that character and ability rather than birth alone make the man was very much in the air at the time, and had already been stated by Confucius.

Mo Tzu's second principle, "identifying with one's superior," is likewise less controversial than it may appear to modern readers in the West. There is a very strong strain of authoritarianism in early Chinese philosophy. Independence of thought and action, for the lower classes at least, is a rarely expressed concept in the works of the period—the only example that comes to mind is Confucius' dictum: "The commander of the forces of a large state may be carried off, but the will of even the common man cannot be taken from him" (*Analects* IX, 25). The Taoists, it is true, talk much of freedom of thought and action, but it is a freedom which ignores or transcends the social order, not one that functions effectively within it. The concept of the hierarchical social order itself, the neat pyramid of classes and functionaries topped by the Son of Heaven, was an ideal that apparently no thinker dreamed of challenging. Therefore when Mo Tzu urges that each group in society must accept its standards of judgment and take orders from the group above it, he is expressing an

assumption common to Mo-ists, Confucians, and, later, Legal-
ists alike. Advice could, and indeed should, flow freely upward in the hierarchy. But decisions, in normal times at least,
come only from above. Each individual and group in society,
if he or it goes morally awry, may thus be checked and cor-
rected by the group above. (Needless to say, Chinese society
did not always function in this way, which explains why Mo
Tzu and others spent so much time expounding this ideal.)

But what happens if the man at the very top goes awry?
The Confucians believed that in that case, and in that case
alone, the normal process may be reversed and a new leader
may rise up from the lower ranks to replace the man at the
top who has, by his misrule, disqualified himself for the position he holds. The new leader is able to do this because of
his superior virtue, which wins for him both the support of
society and the sanction of Heaven. Mo Tzu recognizes the
same process, but pays less attention to the leader himself,
who is only an agent of divine retribution, than to the power
directing the process, the supernatural power of Heaven and
the spirits.

Which brings us to Mo Tzu's religious views. He asserts
that nature spirits and the ghosts of the dead exist, that they
take cognizance of all human activities, and that they have
the power to reward or punish any individual for his deeds.
Heading the hierarchy of the supernatural world he envisions
a deity called God, the Lord on High, or Heaven, who creates
all beings, loves all beings, and desires their welfare, working
towards that end through the earthly representatives of the
deity, the Son of Heaven and his officers. There is nothing
novel about such views; they are striking only as a reaffirma-
tion of traditional religious beliefs. If we turn to the *Odes* and
Documents, we will find such assumptions underlying almost

every line, while the mass of early historical legends preserved in the *Tso chuan* abounds in stories of spirits who returned from the land of the dead to take personal revenge
upon their enemies. Yet the very insistence with which Mo
Tzu proclaims these beliefs indicates that they had lost, or
were losing, their hold on the men of his generation, at least
those of the ruling class, the audience to which his words are
addressed. The Confucians, recognizing and even encouraging
this trend toward skepticism and agnosticism, worked to sal-
vage and revitalize the old religious rites and forms by imbu-
ing them with new interpretations that were more in keeping
with the changing intellectual climate of the time. Mo Tzu,
on the other hand, attacked the trend of the times head on,
and attempted to drag men back to the simple, pietistic, and
fear-ridden faith of antiquity. For only through such a faith,
he believed, could men be frightened into abandoning their
evil ways and persuaded to love and benefit one another as
Heaven desired them to.

The doctrine of universal love is the most famous and original of Mo Tzu's contributions to Chinese thought. We have
already noted the negative side of it in his condemnations of
offensive warfare, condemnations which could just as well
have been made by thinkers of the Confucian or Taoist
schools. But Mo Tzu alone of all Chinese thinkers was not
content merely to condemn acts that are harmful to others.
He went a step further to proclaim that men should actually
love the members of other families and states in the same way
that they love the members of their own family and state, for
all are equally the creatures and people of God.

This is a noble and original ideal indeed, especially when
we consider the fierce strife and hatred that characterized the
society of Mo Tzu's time. Here at last is a man who dared to

look beyond the hierarchical and geographical divisions of feudal society to a view of all mankind united in fellowship and love. When we examine the arguments which Mo Tzu puts forward to support such an ideal, however, we can understand, at least in part, why it was for so many centuries neglected or even scoffed at by the Chinese.

In the form of an imaginary dialogue, Mo Tzu presents the objections which he believes his opponents will raise to his doctrine of universal love, and answers them one by one. In brief summary, this is how his argument runs:

Q. What good is such a doctrine?

A. It will bring the greatest benefit to the largest number of people.

Q. Can it be put into practice?

A. Yes. This is proved by the fact that it actually *was* practiced by the sage kings of antiquity.

Q. How is it to be put into practice?

A. The rulers can be persuaded of its usefulness, and they in turn will enforce it among the people by laws and coercion.

The society of Mo Tzu's day, with its local prides and strong sense of family solidarity, could not be expected to respond with much sympathy to such a call for universal altruism and love. The need for a more pious and fearful regard for the spirits, for frugal living, for cessation of costly aggressive warfare—these were ideals all men could comprehend, though they might not agree with them. But a doctrine as novel as that of universal love was bound to be met with bafflement and ridicule. It alone among Mo Tzu's ideas does not seem to have been a commonplace of the thought of his time, or to hark back to older beliefs of ancient Chinese society.

On the contrary it is a startling, original, and even revolutionary concept, and we might expect that Mo Tzu, when putting it forward, would attempt to support it with arguments that are as lofty and challenging as the ideal itself, to clothe it with some sort of poetry or rhetoric that would help the listener to believe that it was in fact attainable, or at least worth striving for. And yet, as we have seen, he defends it in exactly the same pedestrian and uninspired way in which he defends every other doctrine he preaches—by an appeal to material benefit, to authoritarianism, and to the dubious account of an ancient golden age. Perhaps he felt that only such (in his eyes) hardheaded and practical arguments could mask the visionary idealism of the doctrine itself and make it palatable to his hearers. Yet nowhere is the reader likely to feel more strongly the contrast, characteristic of Mo Tzu's thought as a whole, between the essential loftiness of his doctrines, and the plodding, matter-of-fact, and (in modern eyes) often painfully inadequate arguments by which he supports them. Moreover, the arguments delimit and qualify the ideals to such an extent that they end by dragging them down to their own level of cautious utilitarianism, and piety, nonaggression, and universal love become no more than judicious policies of government.

These, then, are the principal doctrines of Mo Tzu and his followers. And how did such doctrines fare in the world of ancient China? It is customary to cite in answer the alarmed statement of Mencius, recorded in *Mencius* III B, ch. 9, that "The words of Yang Chu and Mo Ti fill the world!" Yang Chu, another philosopher of the time, seems to have taught a rather extreme every-man-for-himself doctrine which Mencius believed posed, along with the universal love doctrine of Mo Tzu, the greatest threat to the Confucian concept of unselfish but carefully graded benevolence and kindness toward others. It would seem, therefore, that the teachings of Mo Tzu had attained considerable vogue in Mencius' time, though Mencius, like so many thinkers, probably has a tendency to exaggerate the over-all potency of philosophical ideas as a whole, and of those of his enemies in particular. It should also be noted that Mencius lived in the same northeastern area of China where Mo Tzu had lived and taught, and where Mo Tzu's ideas could be expected to have the strongest following.

Nevertheless, other works of the third century in addition to the *Mencius* suggest that Mo-ism at this period stood side by side with Confucianism as one of the most important philosophical schools of the time. And yet, from the second century on, after the unification of the empire under the Ch'in and later the Han dynasties, though Mo-ism is still mentioned as a system of thought, we hear nothing more of the Mo-ist school and its followers. What became of them?

Mencius, in the passage cited above, after commenting on the disturbing prevalence of Mo-ist ideas, proceeds to a biased and cursory rebuttal of them, claiming that Mo Tzu's doctrine of universal love is equivalent to "being without a father"; that is, it violates the Confucian concept of a graded love that is strongest for one's own relatives and friends and weaker for those less closely related by blood or association. Some scholars tend to regard this brief attack of Mencius as the blow that killed Mo-ism, though this is surely to invest the words of Mencius with far more weight and authority than they ever possessed in the intellectual world of ancient China. In later centuries, when Mencius was hailed as the true interpreter of Confucianism and the *Mencius* became a classic, such a pronouncement may have effectively discouraged any revival of interest in Mo Tzu and his ideas. But in the second and first centuries B.C. it could hardly have killed off the Mo-ist school.

What killed Mo-ism, I believe, was the fact that profound changes in Chinese society and intellectual life rendered so many of its tenets unappealing to the members of the ruling class, the audience to which it was primarily directed.

In the centuries following Mo Tzu's death, technological progress in agriculture and industry and the growth of trade made the life of the upper classes far more affluent than it had been in his day, and they were less inclined than ever to listen to sermons on frugality and plain living. At the same time, a growing atmosphere of sophistication and rationalism led men to reject or radically reinterpret the ancient legends and religious beliefs that Mo Tzu had so fervently affirmed. The common people probably continued to hold fast to the old beliefs, and indeed the idea of the retribution of the spirits reappears, as vigorous as ever, among the tenets of popular Taoism in the second century A.D. But educated men of the Ch'in and Han no doubt cast a skeptical eye on Mo Tzu's tales of vengeful ghosts. Finally, the bald utilitarianism with which he supported his doctrines, though a cogent argument in narrowly political concerns, was felt to be an inadequate basis for an entire system of moral philosophy. Beside Confucian ethics or the metaphysics of Taoism, it held little attraction for the men of an urbane and aesthetic-minded society.

The author of a late chapter of the *Chuang Tzu*, commenting upon the dour Mo-ist philosophy which allows "no singing in life, no mourning in death," remarks: "It causes the people to be anxious, to be sorrowful, and its ways are hard to follow" (*Chuang Tzu*, ch. 10, "T'ien-hsia"). This, we may suppose, was how most men of later centuries felt about the puritanical and superstitious elements of Mo Tzu's teachings. What remained—his emphasis upon selecting and promoting worthy men to office, upon the welfare of the people, upon pacifism and benevolent authoritarianism—was perfectly compatible, and in fact almost identical, with traditional Confucian teachings, and could therefore be easily absorbed in the Confucian school. Thus we find writers of the second and first centuries B.C. talking about *Ju-Mo*, "the doctrines of the Confucians and Mo-ists," not as though they were two fiercely rival systems of thought, but as though they were synonymous, or at least complementary.[2]

One more reason may be suggested for the decline of the Mo-ist school and the indifference of later ages to its doctrines. This is the nature of the work in which its ideas have been preserved, the *Mo Tzu*, particularly those portions described above which deal with Mo Tzu's own doctrines. We do not know exactly when these chapters were written, but it is probable that they represent one of the earliest attempts at philosophical writing in Chinese, preceded only by the fragmentary *Analects*. In view of this, it is perhaps unfair to compare the book with the more subtle, individualistic and polished works of the following century, such as the *Chuang Tzu*, *Hsün Tzu*, and *Han Fei Tzu*. Nevertheless, making allowances for its antiquity, one cannot help noting that the *Mo Tzu*, whatever the interest of its ideas, is seldom a delight to read. Its arguments are almost always presented in an orderly

[2] So completely did Confucian ideas come to dominate the outlook of educated Chinese that, when scholars of the present century began once more to study Mo Tzu's philosophy, they found his religious views so radically "un-Chinese" that they were led to postulate a foreign origin for them. With more conviction than scholarship, they variously asserted that Mo Tzu was an Indian Buddhist, a Brahmin, or a Moslem from Arabia (!). For a convenient survey of these and other theories on the origin of the Mo-ist school, see the article in Chinese, "Mo-chia yüan-liu pien (I)," by Lu Kuang-huan, *World Forum*, II (nos. 5–6, 1961), 2–5.

and lucid, if not logically convincing, fashion. But the style as a whole is marked by a singular monotony of sentence pattern, and a lack of wit or grace that is atypical of Chinese literature in general. *Han Fei Tzu,* sec. 32, records an anecdote in which a ruler of the time questions a Mo-ist scholar on the reason for the flat, unadorned style of the work. The Mo-ist replies with a parable intimating that, if a writer employs too florid and engaging a style, his readers are apt to become so dazzled by the rhetoric that they lose sight of what is being said. Whatever one may think of the validity of this assertion, it is quite possible that the Mo-ists did deliberately adopt a straightforward, bare style for just such reasons. The extreme repetitiousness of the work, for example, suggests that the writer or writers are not repeating themselves merely out of paucity of invention, but are attempting purposely to drum certain set phrases into the mind of the reader, much like the slogan-vendors of our own time.[3]

When translating an author whose style is genuinely interesting and varied, the translator may perhaps be justified in disguising minor lapses and redundancies when he brings the work over into another language. But when repetitiousness constitutes the main feature of the style of the original, he can be faithful to the ethics of his trade, it would seem, only by reproducing such repetitions in full in the translation. This I have done, trusting that the reader will soon come to recognize the clusters of set phrases which, like patterns in a cloth, reappear again and again in the text.

[3] An extreme example of this is the slogan "Making music is wrong!" which Mo Tzu employs as a kind of refrain throughout his chapter attacking music. When the Confucian philosopher Hsün Tzu wrote a rebuttal to Mo Tzu's arguments, he parodied this feature of Mo Tzu's style by using a refrain of his own, "And yet Mo Tzu criticizes it. Why?" (*Hsün Tzu,* sec. 20).

In addition to this flatness of style, the *Mo Tzu* has been made even more taxing to read by the long neglect which the text has suffered. Whereas almost all other important works of early Chinese philosophy and literature had at least one commentary appended to them by the third or fourth century A.D., the *Mo Tzu* did not enjoy this attention until some fifteen hundred years later. Meanwhile the text, difficult enough to comprehend without a commentary, fell into worse and worse condition at the hands of careless and baffled copyists. It is only in recent years that scholars have succeeded in untangling most of the garbles and elucidating the meaning to a reasonably satisfactory extent. The very repetitiousness of the text has considerably aided their efforts, since a passage which is corrupt in one section can often be restored from an uncorrupted parallel passage elsewhere. Nevertheless, many passages remain which cannot, without extensive and sometimes questionable emendation, be made to yield any sense at all. This is particularly true of Mo Tzu's frequent quotations from lost sections of the *Book of Documents*, which are in archaic style. Even where he quotes from sections of the *Documents* or *Odes* that are preserved today, we cannot be sure how he interpreted the passages he quotes. As pointed out in the notes, my translation is therefore in many places highly tentative.

In the translation I have followed the text given in the *Mo Tzu chien-ku* by Sun I-jang (1848–1908), reprinted by Chung-hua shu-chü (Shanghai, 1954), which is generally acknowledged to be the most reliable text and commentary. I have also profited by the *Mo Tzu hsin-cheng* (preface dated 1938) by Yü Hsing-wu; the Japanese translation by Koyanagi Shigeta in the Kokuyaku kambun taisei series (Tokyo, 1920);

and the English translation of these sections of the *Mo Tzu* by Yi-pao Mei, *The Ethical and Political Works of Motse*, Probsthain's Oriental Series, vol. XIX (London, 1929). I am particularly indebted to the last for many valuable suggestions on how to render Mo Tzu in English. Other important recent works on the *Mo Tzu* are listed below.

Mê Ti, Alfred Forke. Berlin, 1922. Complete German translation of *Mo Tzu*.

Mo Tzu ching-chi ssu-hsiang, Hsiung Meng. Peking, 1925. On Mo Tzu's economic thought.

Mo Tzu chi-chieh, Chang Ch'un-i. Shanghai, 1932. Commentary.

Mo Tzu shih-pu, Liu Shih-p'ei; in *Liu Shen-shu hsien-sheng i-shu*, 1934. Commentary.

Bokushi, Kobayashi Ichirō. 2 vols. Keisho daikō series #16–17. Tokyo, 1938–39. Japanese translation and commentary.

Bokushi no kenkyū, Ōtsuka Banroku. Tokyo, 1943. A study of the *Mo Tzu*.

Mo Tzǔ, Harvard-Yenching Institute Sinological Index Series, Supplement #21. 1948; reprinted 1961.

Mo Tzu yen-chiu lun-wen chi, Luan T'iao-fu. Peking, 1957. Collection of essays on various aspects of the *Mo Tzu*.

Special studies of the *Mo-ching* or chapters on logic:

Mo-ching chiao-shih, Liang Ch'i-ch'ao. Shanghai, 1922. Commentary.

Mo-ching t'ung-chieh, Chang Ch'i-huang. Peking, 1931. Commentary.

Mo-pien shu-cheng, Fan Keng-yen. Shanghai, 1935. Commentary.

Mo-ching chiao-ch'üan, Kao Heng. Peking, 1958. Commentary.

Mo-pien fa-wei, T'an Chieh-fu. Peking, 1958. Commentary.

Special study of Mo Tzu's chapters on military science:

Mo Tzu ch'eng-shou ko-p'ien chien-chu, Ts'en Chung-mien. Peking, 1958. Commentary.

HONORING THE WORTHY
PART I
(SECTION 8)

Master Mo Tzu[1] said: These days the rulers and high officials who govern the nation all desire their states to be rich, their population numerous, and their administration well ordered. And yet what they achieve is not wealth but poverty, not a numerous population but a meager one, not order but chaos. In actual fact, they fail to get what they seek and instead achieve what they abhor. Why is this?

Mo Tzu said: It is because the rulers and high officials who govern the nation fail to honor the worthy and employ the capable in their administration. If a government is rich in worthy men, then the administration will be characterized by weight and substance; but if it is poor in such men, then the administration will be a paltry affair. Therefore the task confronting the high officials is simply to increase the number of worthy men. But what means are to be used to increase the number of worthy men?

Mo Tzu said: Let us suppose that one wishes to increase the number of skilled archers and chariot drivers in the state. One must set about enriching and honoring such men, respecting and praising them. Once this has been done, one will have no difficulty in obtaining a multitude of them. How

[1] This title, Tzu Mo Tzu (Master Mo Tzu), is repeated innumerable times in the text. For the sake of brevity, I shall hereafter translate it simply as "Mo Tzu."

much more appropriate, therefore, that one should do this for worthy men, who are ardent in the practice of virtue, skilled in discourse, and broad in learning! Men such as these are the treasures of the nation and the keepers of its altars of the soil and grain. They too should be enriched and honored, respected and praised, and when this has been done, they may be obtained in plenty.

Therefore, when the sage kings of ancient times administered their states, they announced: "The unrighteous shall not be enriched, the unrighteous shall not be exalted, the unrighteous shall be no kin to us, the unrighteous shall not be our intimates!" When the rich and exalted men of the kingdom heard this, they all began to deliberate among themselves, saying, "We have trusted in our wealth and exalted position, but now the lord promotes the righteous without caring whether they are poor or humble. We too, then, must become righteous." Likewise the kin of the ruler began to deliberate, saying, "We have trusted in the bond of kinship, but now the lord promotes the righteous without caring how distant the relationship. We too, then, must become righteous." Those who were intimate with the ruler deliberated, saying, "We have trusted in the intimacy we enjoyed, but now the lord promotes the righteous without caring how far removed they may have been from him until now. We too, then, must become righteous." And when those who were far removed from the ruler heard it, they also deliberated, saying, "We used to believe that, since we were so far removed from the ruler, we had nothing to trust in. But now the lord promotes the righteous without caring how far removed they may be. We too, then, must become righteous." So the vassals of distant and outlying areas, as well as the noblemen's sons serving in the palace, the multitudes of the capital, and the peasants of the four borders, in time came to hear of this, and all strove to become righteous.

Why did the ancient kings do this? Those in a superior position have one thing by which to attract men to their service—the promise of material benefits; those in a subordinate position have one thing to offer to their superiors—a knowledge of the arts of government. Let us suppose there is a rich man who has built a high wall all around his house. When the wall is finished and plastered with mud, he pierces it with only one gate. Then, if a thief steals in, he may shut the gate by which the thief entered and set about searching for him, confident that the thief has no means of escape. Why? Because the rich man, like the ruler, has control of the vital point.

Therefore in their administration the sage kings of ancient times ranked the virtuous high and honored the worthy, and although a man might be a farmer or an artisan from the shops, if he had ability they promoted him. Such men were honored with titles, treated to generous stipends, entrusted with important matters, and empowered to see that their orders were carried out. For it was said that if their stipends were not generous, the people would have no confidence in them; and if their orders were not carried out, the people would not stand in awe of them. These three benefits were bestowed upon the worthy not because the ruler wished to reward them for their worth but because he hoped thereby to bring about success in the affairs of government. Therefore at that time ranks were assigned according to virtue, duties allotted according to the office held, and rewards given according to the effort expended; achievements were weighed and stipends distributed accordingly. Thus no official was necessarily assured of an exalted position for life, nor was any member of the common people

necessarily condemned to remain forever humble. Those with
ability were promoted, those without it were demoted. This is
what it means to promote public righteousness and do away
with private likes and dislikes.

In ancient times Yao raised up Shun from the sunny side of
Fu Lake and entrusted the government to him, and the world
was at peace. Yü raised up Yi from the land of Yin and entrusted the government to him, and the nine provinces were
well ordered. T'ang raised up Yi Yin from his labors in the
kitchen and entrusted the government to him, and his plans
were successful. King Wen raised up Hung-yao T'ai-tien from
his place among the hunting and fishing nets and entrusted
the government to him, and the western regions bowed in sub-
mission.[2]

So among the officials who enjoyed high ranks and generous
stipends in those days, there were none who were not un-
failingly cautious and respectful, none who did not encourage
and strive with each other in honoring virtue. It is gentlemen
of true worth, therefore, who must act to assist and carry on
the government. If the ruler can obtain the services of such
gentlemen, then his plans will never be thwarted nor his body
worn by care; his fame will be established and his undertak-
ings brought to a successful conclusion; his excellence will be
manifest and no evil will appear to mar it. All this will come
about because he has obtained the services of gentlemen.

Therefore Mo Tzu said: When things are going well, gen-

[2] Yao, Shun, Yü, T'ang, and King Wen were all ancient sage rulers, the
last three the founders of the Hsia, Shang, and Chou dynasties respectively,
the so-called Three Dynasties. Yi of the land of Yin was an eminent minister of Shun and Yü. Yi Yin was supposed to have been working in
T'ang's royal kitchens when his worth was recognized. The identity of
Hung-yao T'ai-tien and the anecdote upon which Mo Tzu's statement is
based are unknown.

tlemen of worth must be promoted; and when they are not going well, gentlemen of worth must be promoted. If one wishes to emulate and carry on the ways of Yao, Shun, Yü, and T'ang, then one must honor the worthy, for honoring the worthy is the foundation of good government.

PART II

(SECTION 9)

Mo Tzu said: In caring for the people, presiding over the altars of the soil and grain, and ordering the state, the rulers and high officials these days strive for stability and seek to avoid any error. But why do they fail to perceive that honoring the worthy is the foundation of government?

How do we know that honoring the worthy is the foundation of government? Because when the eminent and wise rule over the stupid and humble, then there will be order; but when the stupid and humble rule over the eminent and wise, there will be chaos. Therefore we know that honoring the worthy is the foundation of government.

Therefore the sage kings of ancient times took great pains to honor the worthy and employ the capable, showing no special consideration for their own kin, no partiality for the eminent and rich, no favoritism for the good-looking and attractive. They promoted the worthy to high places, enriched and honored them, and made them heads of government; the unworthy they demoted and rejected, reduced to poverty and humble station, and condemned to penal servitude. Thus the people, encouraged by the hope of reward and awed by the fear of punishment, led each other on to become worthy, so that worthy men increased in number and unworthy men became few. This is what is called advancing the worthy. And when this had been done, the sage kings listened to the words of the worthy, watched their actions, observed their abilities, and on this basis carefully assigned them to office. This is called employing the capable. Those who were capable of ordering the state were employed to order the state; those who were capable of heading a government bureau were employed as heads of bureaus; and those who were capable of governing an outlying district were employed to govern the outlying districts. Thus the administration of the state, of the government bureaus, and of the outlying districts was in every case in the hands of the most worthy men of the nation.

When a worthy man is given the task of ordering the state, he appears at court early and retires late, listens to lawsuits and attends to the affairs of government. As a result the state is well ordered and laws and punishments are justly administered. When a worthy man heads a government bureau, he goes to bed late and gets up early, collecting taxes on the barriers and markets and on the resources of the hills, forests, lakes, and fish weirs, so that the treasury will be full. As a result the treasury is full and no source of revenue is neglected. When a worthy man governs an outlying district, he leaves his house early and returns late, plowing and sowing seed, planting trees, and gathering vegetables and grain.[3] As a result there will be plenty of vegetables and grain and the people will have enough to eat. When the state is well ordered, the

---

[3] The text reads as though the officials of the outlying districts actually go out and work in the fields, which seems highly unlikely. The probable meaning is that they supervise the work of the peasants. Mo Tzu, like many earlier Chinese writers, is sometimes betrayed by his fondness for strict verbal parallelism into saying something other than just what he means.

laws and punishments will be justly administered, and when the treasury is full, the people will be well off. The rulers will thus be supplied with wine and millet to use in their sacrifices to Heaven and the spirits, with hides and currency to use in their intercourse with the feudal lords of neighboring states, and with the means to feed the hungry and give rest to the weary within their realm, to nourish their subjects and attract virtuous men from all over the world. Then Heaven and the spirits will send down riches, the other feudal lords will become their allies, the people of their own realm will feel affection for them, and worthy men will come forward to serve them. Thus all that they plan for they will achieve, and all that they undertake will be brought to a successful conclusion. If they stay within their realm, their position will be secure, and if they venture forth to punish an enemy, they will be victorious. It was by this method alone that the sage kings of the Three Dynasties, Yao, Shun, Yü, T'ang, Wen, and Wu, were able to rule the world and become the leaders of the other lords.

But if one knows only the policy to be adopted, but does not know what means to use in carrying it out, then he cannot be sure of success in government. Therefore three principles should be established. What are these three principles? They are that if the titles and positions of worthy men are not exalted enough, then the people will not respect such men; if their stipends are not generous, then the people will not have confidence in them; and if their orders are not enforced, then the people will not stand in awe of them. Therefore the sage kings of antiquity honored the worthy with titles, treated them to generous stipends, entrusted them with important affairs, and empowered them to see that their orders were carried out. These benefits were bestowed not bcause the ruler wished to reward his ministers, but because he hoped thereby to bring about success in the affairs of government.

The *Book of Odes* says:

> I admonish you to take thought for the needy;
> I teach you how to assign the titles;
> For who can take hold of something hot
> Without first moistening his hand?[4]

This verse shows how important it was for the rulers and lords of antiquity to secure good men to be their ministers and aides, and compares this to the necessity of moistening the hand before grasping anything hot so as to spare the hand from injury.

Thus the sage kings of antiquity gave all their thought to finding worthy men and employing them, handing out titles to honor them, apportioning lands to enfeoff them, and never to the end of their days stinting their efforts. Worthy men for their part thought only of finding an enlightened lord and serving him, exhausting the strength of their four limbs in carrying out their lord's business, never to the end of their days growing weary, and if they achieved anything that was beautiful or good, they gave credit for it to the ruler. Thus all that was beautiful and good came to reside in the ruler, while all grudges and complaints were directed against his subordinates. Peace and joy was the portion of the ruler, care and sorrow that of his ministers. This was how the sage kings of ancient times administered their rule.

Now the rulers and high officials of the present day attempt to imitate the ancients in honoring the worthy and employing the capable in their governments. But although they honor them with titles, the stipends which they allot to them do

---

[4] *Ta ya* section, "Sang jou" (Mao text no. 257).

not follow in proportion. Now if an official has a high-sounding title but a meager stipend, he can hardly inspire the confidence of the people. Such an official will say to himself, "The ruler does not really appreciate me, but is only making use of me as a means for his own ends." And how can men who feel that they are being made use of ever have any affection for their superiors? Therefore the kings of antiquity used to say: "He who is greedy for power in government can never bring himself to assign responsibility to others, and he who is too fond of wealth can never bring himself to dole out stipends." And if one refuses to delegate responsibility or dole out stipends, though one invites all the worthy men of the world, what inducement will they have to come to the side of the ruler and his officers?

If the worthy do not come to the side of the ruler and his officers, it will be the unworthy who will wait at their left and right, and when the unworthy wait upon their left and right, then praise will not be meted out to the worthy and censure to the wicked. If the ruler honors unworthy men such as these and uses them in governing the state, then rewards will not necessarily find their way into the hands of the worthy, and punishments will not necessarily fall upon those who deserve them. If the worthy are not rewarded and the wicked are not punished, then there will be no way to encourage the worthy or put a stop to evil. Unworthy men such as these are not loving or filial to their parents at home nor respectful and friendly to the people of their neighborhood. Their actions show no sense of propriety, their comings and goings no sense of restraint, and their relations with the opposite sex no sense of decorum. Put in charge of a government bureau, they steal and plunder; assigned to guard a city, they betray their trust or rebel. If their lord encounters difficulty, they will not accompany him into exile. When they are as-signed the task of hearing lawsuits, their judgments are not apt; when they are given that of apportioning wealth, their allotments are not equitable. With men such as these to work with, the ruler's plans will reach no fulfillment and his under-takings no success. Though he stays within his realm, he will know no security, and if he ventures forth to battle, he will win no victory. It was for this reason alone that the evil kings of the Three Dynasties, Chieh, Chou, Yu, and Li, lost their kingdoms and brought destruction to their altars of the soil and grain.[5]

All of this comes about as a result of understanding petty affairs but failing to understand important ones. Now the rulers and high officials know that if they cannot cut a suit of clothes for themselves, they must employ the services of a skilled tailor, and if they cannot slaughter an ox or a sheep for themselves, they must employ the services of a skilled butcher. In these two instances the rulers are perfectly aware of the need to honor worthy men and employ the capable to get things done. And yet when they see the state in confusion and their altars of the soil and grain in danger, they do not know enough to employ capable men to correct the situation. Instead they employ their relatives, or men who happen to be rich and eminent or pleasant-featured and attractive. But just because a man happens to be rich and eminent or pleasant-featured and attractive, he will not necessarily turn out to be wise and alert when placed in office. If men such as these are

---

[5] Chieh was the last ruler of the Hsia dynasty, Chou the last ruler of the Shang, and Yu and Li two rulers of the Chou dynasty in the 9th and 8th centuries B.C. All four are symbols of evil and incompetent rulers.

given the task of ordering the state, then this is simply to entrust the state to men who are neither wise nor intelligent, and anyone knows that this will lead to ruin.

Moreover, the rulers and high officials trust a man's mental ability because they are attracted by his looks, and treat him with affection without bothering to examine his knowledge. As a result a man who is incapable of taking charge of a hundred persons is assigned to a post in charge of a thousand, and a man who is incapable of taking charge of a thousand persons is assigned to a post in charge of ten thousand. Why do the rulers do this? Because if they assign a man they like to such a post, he will receive an exalted title and a generous stipend. Hence they employ the man simply because they are attracted by his looks.

Now if a man who is incapable of taking charge of a thousand persons is given a post in charge of ten thousand, then he is being given a post that requires ten times what he is capable of. Affairs of government arise every day and must be attended to each day, and yet the day cannot be made ten times longer for the sake of such a man. Furthermore, it takes knowledge to attend to such affairs, but if the man's knowledge cannot be increased tenfold and he is still assigned to a post that requires ten times what he is capable of, then it will result in his attending to one matter and neglecting nine others. Though the man works day and night to attend to the duties of his post, it is obvious that they will never be attended to. All of this comes about because the rulers and high officials do not understand how to honor the worthy and employ the capable in their government.

Earlier I described the method for honoring the worthy and employing the capable in government so as to achieve order, and here I have described how rejecting the worthy and failing to employ the capable in government leads to chaos. Now if the rulers and high officials truly wish to order the state properly, to achieve stability and avoid error, why do they fail to perceive that honoring the worthy is the foundation of good government?

Moreover, this principle, that honoring the worthy is the foundation of government, is not something asserted by Mo Tzu alone. It is the way of the sage kings, and is found recorded in the books of the former kings and embodied in the sayings which have been handed down from antiquity. Thus one book says: "Seek out sages and wise men to protect and aid you!" And the "Oath of T'ang" states: "Then I sought out a great sage with whom to unite my strength and join my mind in governing the empire." [6] These quotations show that the sages did not fail to honor the worthy and employ the capable in their government. Thus the sage kings of ancient times gave all their attention to this problem alone, and did not allow themselves to become distracted by other affairs, and all the world enjoyed the benefits thereof.

In ancient times Shun farmed at Mount Li, made pottery on the banks of the river, and fished at Thunder Lake. Yao discovered him on the sunny side of Fu Lake and promoted him to the position of Son of Heaven, turning over to him the task of ruling the empire and governing the people. Yi Chih served in the bridal party of the daughter of the Hsin clan when she went to marry T'ang, and by his own wish became a cook in T'ang's kitchens. There T'ang discovered him and made him his chief minister, turning over to him the task of ruling the empire and governing the people. Fu Yüeh,

---

[6] The "Oath of T'ang" is one of the sections of the *Book of Documents*, but no such passage is found in the present text of that section. The source of the preceding quotation is unknown.

wearing a coarse robe and a girdle of rope, was working as a convict laborer at Fu-yen when Wu-ting discovered him and made him one of the three highest officers, turning over to him the task of ruling the empire and governing the people.

How did it happen that these men started out in humble positions and ended in exalted ones, began in poverty and ended in riches? Because the rulers and their high officials understood the importance of honoring the worthy and employing the capable. So among their people were none who were hungry and yet found no food, cold and yet found no clothing, weary and yet found no rest; there were none who were disorderly and yet in time did not learn obedience.

The ancient sage kings, in giving all their thought to honoring the worthy and employing the capable in government, were patterning their actions on the ways of Heaven. For Heaven too shows no discrimination between rich and poor, eminent and humble, near and far, the closely and the distantly related. It promotes and honors the worthy, and demotes and rejects the unworthy.

If this is so, then who were those that, possessing wealth and eminence, still strove to be worthy, and received their reward? The sage kings of the Three Dynasties of old, Yao, Shun, Yü, T'ang, Wen, and Wu, were such. And how were they rewarded? When they ruled the world, they loved all men universally, worked to benefit them, and taught their subjects to honor Heaven and serve the spirits. Because they loved and benefited their subjects, Heaven and the spirits rewarded them by setting them up as Sons of Heaven and causing them to act as fathers and mothers to the people. The people in turn praised them, calling them sage kings, and so they are called even today. These then were the rich and eminent ones who strove to be worthy and who received their reward.

Who were those that, possessing wealth and eminence, still practiced evil, and were punished for it? The wicked kings of the Three Dynasties of old, Chieh, Chou, Yu, and Li, were such. How do we know that this is so? Because when they ruled the world, they hated all men universally, set about to oppress them, and taught the people of the world to curse Heaven and abuse the spirits. Because they oppressed and tyrannized their subjects, Heaven and the spirits punished them by bringing execution and death to their persons, scattering their sons and grandsons, destroying their houses, and cutting off their descendants. The people accordingly condemned them, calling them wicked kings, and so they are called even today. These then were the rich and eminent ones who practiced evil and who were punished for it.

Who was it that, though closely related to the ruler, failed to do good and was punished for it? Such was Lord Kun, the eldest son of the emperor.[7] He turned his back on the virtuous ways of the emperor and so was banished to the fields of Yü and imprisoned where no warmth nor light could reach him, and the emperor showed him no favor. He, then, was one who, though closely related to the ruler, failed to do good and was punished for it.

Who were the capable ones who were employed by Heaven? Such were Yü, Chi, and Kao T'ao.[8] How do we know that this is so? Because among the documents of the former kings is the "Penal Code of Lü," which says: "The august emperor carefully inquired among the lower people, and there were

---

[7] Various accounts are given of this mythical figure. According to the one which Mo Tzu appears to be following, he was the son of a ruler named Chuan Hsü. It is not clear whether Chuan Hsü himself, or one of his successors, banished Lord Kun.

[8] These men were all said to have been enlightened ministers under the sage Shun. In the quotation from the *Book of Documents* which follows, however, Kao T'ao is not mentioned, but instead Po Yi, another eminent minister of Shun.

complaints against the Miao barbarians. . . . The attention of the various lords was extended among the lower people and they brought to light the enlightened, no matter who they were, so that even widowers and widows were not left unrecognized. The virtuous might of the sovereign overawed the people; his virtuous enlightenment made them bright. Then he charged three lords to be zealous in doing good for the people. Po Yi handed down the statutes, restraining the people with punishments. Yü regulated the water and the land and presided over the naming of the hills and rivers. Chi descended from his high position to sow seed and teach the people to grow fine grain. When these three lords had completed their work, the people were greatly benefited." [9]

The three sages mentioned in this passage were careful in their words, circumspect in their actions, and thorough in their thoughts and plans. They sought to discover every hidden matter in the world, every benefit that had previously been overlooked. They served Heaven above, and Heaven responded to their virtue. They acted for the sake of the people below, and the people received benefit their whole life through.

Thus the former kings used to say: "This Way! Use it on a grand scale throughout the world and it will never prove too petty; use it on a small scale and it will never prove confining; use it for a long time and the people will benefit their whole lives through." The hymns of Chou speak of it in these words:

> The virtue of the sage
> Is high as heaven,

[9] From the *Lü hsing,* or "Penal Code of Lü," in the *Book of Documents.* On the whole I have followed the interpretation of Karlgren, though for "they brought to light the enlightened, no matter who they were," he reads "clearly elucidated the irregular practices (*sc.* punishments)." In most cases we can only guess from context how Mo Tzu himself interpreted the passages which he quotes from the *Odes* and *Documents.*

Broad as the earth;
It shines upon the world,
Solid as the ground,
Lofty as the mountains,
Never faltering, never failing,
Brilliant like the sun,
Bright like the moon,
Constant as heaven and earth.[10]

This describes how brilliant, broad, deep-rooted, and ever-lasting is the virtue of the sage. The virtue of the sage may in fact be said to embrace all heaven and earth!

Now the rulers and high officials wish to rule the world and become leaders of the feudal lords. Yet if they are without such virtue and righteousness, what means will they have to achieve their aims? Some say that such aims can be accomplished through a display of might and power, but why should the rulers attempt to display might and power? Those who strive to overthrow others simply drive the people to their death. What the people long for most is life, and what they hate most is death. Yet under such rulers they cannot achieve what they long for, but are subjected in case after case to what they hate. From ancient times down to the present there has never been anyone who succeeded in ruling the world and becoming the leader of the feudal lords in this way. Now the rulers and high officials say they want to rule the world and become leaders of the feudal lords. But if they really wish to have their way with the world and leave behind them a name for future generations to remember, why do they not realize that honoring the worthy is the foundation of good government? This is a principle which the sages were most careful to practice.

[10] No such passage is found among the hymns (*sung*) of Chou preserved in the *Book of Odes*.

IDENTIFYING WITH ONE'S
SUPERIOR
PART I
(SECTION 11)

Mo Tzu said: In ancient times, when mankind was first born and before there were any laws or government, it may be said that every man's view of things was different. One man had one view, two men had two views, ten men had ten views—the more men, the more views. Moreover, each man believed that his own views were correct and disapproved of those of others, so that people spent their time condemning one another. Within the family fathers and sons, older and younger brothers grew to hate each other and the family split up, unable to live in harmony, while throughout the world people all resorted to water, fire, and poison in an effort to do each other injury. Those with strength to spare refused to help out others, those with surplus wealth would let it rot before they would share it, and those with beneficial doctrines to teach would keep them secret and refuse to impart them. The world was as chaotic as though it were inhabited by birds and beasts alone.

To anyone who examined the cause, it was obvious that this chaos came about because of the absence of rulers and leaders. Therefore the most worthy and able man in the world was selected and set up as Son of Heaven.[1] After the Son of Heaven had been set up, because his strength alone was insufficient, other worthy and able men were selected from throughout the world and installed as his three high ministers. After the Son of Heaven and the three high ministers had been set up, because the world was so broad, and because it was not always possible for the ruler and his ministers alone to judge accurately what would be right and profitable for people living in distant countries and strange lands, the world was divided up into countless states, and feudal lords and chiefs were set up to administer them. After the feudal lords and chiefs had been set up, because their strength alone was insufficient, worthy and able men were chosen from the various states to act as their officials.

When all these officials had been installed, the Son of Heaven proclaimed the principle of his rule to the people of the world, saying, "Upon hearing of good or evil, one shall report it to his superior. What the superior considers right all shall consider right; what the superior considers wrong all shall consider wrong. If the superior commits any fault, his subordinates shall remonstrate with him; if his subordinates do good, the superior shall recommend them. To identify oneself with one's superior and not to form cliques on the lower levels—such conduct as this shall be rewarded by those

[1] It is not clear who does the selecting. In the original, the sentence is in the active mood but with no subject expressed, a construction which is perfectly permissible in Chinese but which must be rendered into English in the passive unless the translator chooses to supply a subject. Y. P. Mei supplies the word "Heaven" as the subject and supports this by reference to a parallel passage in sec. 13 (not translated here) which he reads as "Thereupon Heaven wished to unify the standards in the world." But this reading is based on an emendation that does not seem wholly justified. Nevertheless, if pressed, Mo Tzu, like the Confucians, would no doubt say that Heaven, expressing its will through some human or natural agency, did in fact select the Son of Heaven.

above and praised by those below. If, upon hearing of good or evil, one fails to report it to his superior; if what the superior considers right is not accepted as right and what the superior considers wrong is not accepted as wrong; if his subordinates fail to remonstrate with the superior when he commits a fault, or if the superior fails to recommend his subordinates when they do good; if the subordinates make common cause among themselves and fail to identify themselves with their superiors—if there is such conduct as this, it shall be punished by those above and condemned by the people at large." The rulers meted out their rewards and punishments on this basis, examining with the greatest care to make sure that such rewards and punishments were just.

The head of each local community was the most benevolent man in the community, and when he took office, he proclaimed to the people of the community the principle of his rule, saying, "Upon hearing of good or evil, you shall report it to the town head. What the town head considers right all shall consider right; what the town head considers wrong all shall consider wrong. Leave your evil words and imitate the good words of the town head; leave your evil actions and imitate the good actions of the town head!" As long as this command was heeded, how could there be any disorder in the township?

If we examine into the reason why the township was well ordered, we find that it was simply that the town head was able to unify the standards of judgment in the township, and this resulted in order.

The town head was the most benevolent man in the township, and when he took office, he proclaimed to the people in the township the principle of his rule, saying, "Upon hearing of good or evil, you shall report it to the lord of the region.

What the lord considers right all shall consider right; what the lord considers wrong all shall consider wrong. Leave your evil words and imitate the good words of the lord; leave your evil actions and imitate the good actions of the lord!" As long as this command was heeded, how could there be any disorder in the region?

If we examine into the reason why the region was well ordered, we find that it was simply that the lord was able to unify the standards of judgment throughout the region, and this resulted in order.

The lord of the region was the most benevolent man in the region, and when he took office he proclaimed to the people of the region the principle of his rule, saying "Upon hearing good or evil, you shall report it to the Son of Heaven. What the Son of Heaven considers right all shall consider right; what the Son of Heaven considers wrong all shall consider wrong. Leave your evil words and imitate the good words of the Son of Heaven; leave your evil actions and imitate the good actions of the Son of Heaven!" As long as this command was heeded, how could there be any disorder in the world?

If we examine the reason why the world was well ordered, we find that it was simply that the Son of Heaven was able to unify the standards of judgment throughout the world, and this resulted in order.

But although all the people in the world may identify themselves with the Son of Heaven, if they do not also identify themselves with Heaven itself, then calamities will never cease. The violent winds and bitter rains which sweep the world in such profusion these days—these are simply the punishments of Heaven sent down upon the people because they fail to identify themselves with Heaven.

So Mo Tzu said: In ancient times the sage kings devised the five punishments[2] so as to bring order to the people. These were like the main thread binding a skein of silk or the main cord controlling a net, by which the sage kings bound and hauled in those among the people of the world who failed to identify themselves with their superiors.

[2] Various interpretations of the "five punishments" are given in early works, but they are usually considered to be tattooing, cutting off the nose, cutting off the feet, castration, and death.

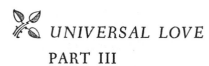

UNIVERSAL LOVE

PART III

(SECTION 16)

Mo Tzu said: It is the business of the benevolent man to try to promote what is beneficial to the world and to eliminate what is harmful. Now at the present time, what brings the greatest harm to the world? Great states attacking small ones, great families overthrowing small ones, the strong oppressing the weak, the many harrying the few, the cunning deceiving the stupid, the eminent lording it over the humble—these are harmful to the world. So too are rulers who are not generous, ministers who are not loyal, fathers who are without kindness, and sons who are unfilial, as well as those mean men who, with weapons, knives, poison, fire, and water, seek to injure and undo each other.

When we inquire into the cause of these various harms, what do we find has produced them? Do they come about from loving others and trying to benefit them? Surely not! They come rather from hating others and trying to injure them. And when we set out to classify and describe those men who hate and injure others, shall we say that their actions are motivated by universality or partiality? Surely we must answer, by partiality, and it is this partiality in their dealings with one another that gives rise to all the great harms in the world. Therefore we know that partiality is wrong.

Mo Tzu said: Whoever criticizes others must have some

alternative to offer them. To criticize and yet offer no alternative is like trying to stop flood with flood or put out fire with fire. It will surely have no effect. Therefore Mo Tzu said: Partiality should be replaced by universality.

But how can partiality be replaced by universality? If men were to regard the states of others as they regard their own, then who would raise up his state to attack the state of another? It would be like attacking his own. If men were to regard the cities of others as they regard their own, then who would raise up his city to attack the city of another? It would be like attacking his own. If men were to regard the families of others as they regard their own, then who would raise up his family to overthrow that of another? It would be like overthrowing his own. Now when states and cities do not attack and make war on each other and families and individuals do not overthrow or injure one another, is this a harm or a benefit to the world? Surely it is a benefit.

When we inquire into the cause of such benefits, what do we find has produced them? Do they come about from hating others and trying to injure them? Surely not! They come rather from loving others and trying to benefit them. And when we set out to classify and describe those men who love and benefit others, shall we say that their actions are motivated by partiality or by universality? Surely we must answer, by universality, and it is this universality in their dealings with one another that gives rise to all the great benefits in the world. Therefore Mo Tzu has said that universality is right.

I have said previously that it is the business of the benevolent man to try to promote what is beneficial to the world and to eliminate what is harmful. Now I have demonstrated that universality is the source of all the great benefits in the world and partiality is the source of all the great harm. It is for this reason that Mo Tzu has said that partiality is wrong and universality is right.

Now if we seek to benefit the world by taking universality as our standard, those with sharp ears and clear eyes will see and hear for others, those with sturdy limbs will work for others, and those with a knowledge of the Way will endeavor to teach others. Those who are old and without wives or children will find means of support and be able to live out their days; the young and orphaned who have no parents will find someone to care for them and look after their needs. When all these benefits may be secured merely by taking universality as our standard, I cannot understand how the men of the world can hear about this doctrine of universality and still criticize it!

And yet the men of the world continue to criticize it, saying, "It may be a good thing, but how can it be put to use?"

Mo Tzu said: If it cannot be put to use, even I would criticize it. But how can there be a good thing that still cannot be put to use? Let us try considering both sides of the question. Suppose there are two men, one of them holding to partiality, the other to universality. The believer in partiality says, "How could I possibly regard my friend the same as myself, or my friend's father the same as my own?" Because he views his friend in this way, he will not feed him when he is hungry, clothe him when he is cold, nourish him when he is sick, or bury him when he dies. Such are the words of the partial man, and such his actions. But the words and actions of the universal-minded man are not like these. He will say, "I have heard that the truly superior man of the world regards his friend the same as himself, and his friend's father the same as his own. Only if he does this can he be considered a truly superior man." Because he views his friend in this way, he will feed him when he is hungry, clothe him when he is cold, nourish him when he is sick, and bury him when he dies. Such are the words and actions of the universal-minded man.

So the words of these two men disagree and their actions are diametrically opposed. Yet let us suppose that both of them are determined to carry out their words in action, so that word and deed agree like the two parts of a tally and nothing they say is not put into action. Then let us venture to inquire further. Suppose that here is a broad plain, a vast wilderness, and a man is buckling on his armor and donning his helmet to set out for the field of battle, where the fortunes of life and death are unknown; or he is setting out in his lord's name upon a distant mission to Pa or Yüeh, Ch'i or Ching, and his return is uncertain. Now let us ask,[1] to whom would he entrust the support of his parents and the care of his wife and children? Would it be to the universal-minded man, or to the partial man? It seems to me that, on occasions like these, there are no fools in the world. Though one may disapprove of universality himself, he would surely think it best to entrust his family to the universal-minded man. Thus people condemn universality in words but adopt it in practice, and word and deed belie each other. I cannot understand how the men of the world can hear about this doctrine of universality and still criticize it!

And yet the men of the world continue to criticize, saying, "Such a principle may be all right as a basis in choosing among ordinary men, but it cannot be used in selecting a ruler."

Let us try considering both sides of the question. Suppose there are two rulers, one of them holding to universality, the

---

[1] The text at this point appears to be corrupt and a few words have been omitted in translation.

other to partiality. The partial ruler says, "How could I possibly regard my countless subjects the same as I regard myself? That would be completely at variance with human nature! Man's life on earth is as brief as the passing of a team of horses glimpsed through a crack in the wall." Because he views his subjects in this way, he will not feed them when they are hungry, clothe them when they are cold, nourish them when they are sick, or bury them when they die. Such are the words of the partial ruler, and such his actions. But the words and actions of the universal-minded ruler are not like these. He will say, "I have heard that the truly enlightened ruler must think of his subjects first, and of himself last. Only then can he be considered a truly enlightened ruler." Because he views his subjects in this way, he will feed them when they are hungry, clothe them when they are cold, nourish them when they are sick, and bury them when they die. Such are the words and actions of the universal-minded ruler.

So the words of these two rulers disagree and their actions are diametrically opposed. Yet let us suppose that both of them speak in good faith and are determined to carry out their words in action, so that word and deed agree like the two parts of a tally and nothing they say is not put into action. Then let us venture to inquire further. Suppose this year there is plague and disease, many of the people are suffering from hardship and hunger, and the corpses of countless victims lie tumbled in the ditches. If the people could choose between these two types of ruler, which would they follow? It seems to me that, on occasions like this, there are no fools in the world. Though one may disapprove of universality himself, he would surely think it best to follow the universal-minded ruler. Thus people condemn universality in words but adopt it in practice, and word and deed belie each other. I cannot understand how the men of the world can hear about this doctrine of universality and still criticize it!

And yet the men of the world continue to criticize, saying, "This doctrine of universality is benevolent and righteous. And yet how can it be carried out? As we see it, one can no more put it into practice than one can pick up Mount T'ai and leap over a river with it! Thus universality is only something to be longed for, not something that can be put into practice."

Mo Tzu said: As for picking up Mount T'ai and leaping over rivers with it, no one from ancient times to the present, from the beginning of mankind to now, has ever succeeded in doing that! But universal love and mutual aid were actually practiced by four sage kings of antiquity. How do we know that they practiced these?

Mo Tzu said: I did not live at the same time as they did, nor have I in person heard their voices or seen their faces. Yet I know it because of what is written on the bamboo and silk that has been handed down to posterity, what is engraved on metal and stone, and what is inscribed on bowls and basins.

The "Great Oath" says: "King Wen was like the sun or moon, shedding his bright light in the four quarters and over the western land." [2] That is to say, the universal love of King Wen was so broad that it embraced the whole world, as the universal light of the sun and the moon shines upon the whole world without partiality. Such was the universality of King Wen, and the universality which Mo Tzu has been telling you about is patterned after that of King Wen.

[2] The "Great Oath," supposedly a speech by King Wu, the son of King Wen, was a section of the *Book of Documents*. It was lost long ago, and the text by that name included in the present *Book of Documents* is a forgery of the 3d century A.D., though it includes a passage much like the one quoted here by Mo Tzu.

Not only the "Great Oath" but the "Oath of Yü" [3] also expresses this idea. Yü said: "All you teeming multitudes, listen to my words! It is not that I, the little child, would dare to act in a disorderly way. But this ruler of the Miao, with his unyielding ways, deserves Heaven's punishment. So I shall lead you, the lords of the various states, to conquer the ruler of the Miao." When Yü went to conquer the ruler of the Miao, it was not that he sought to increase his wealth or eminence, to win fortune or blessing, or to delight his ears and eyes. It was only that he sought to promote what was beneficial to the world and to eliminate what was harmful. Such was the universality of Yü, and the universality which Mo Tzu has been telling you about is patterned after that of Yü.

And not only the "Oath of Yü" but the "Speech of T'ang" [4] also expresses this idea. T'ang said: "I, the little child, Lü, dare to sacrifice a dark beast and make this announcement to the Heavenly Lord above, saying, 'Now Heaven has sent a great drought and it has fallen upon me, Lü. But I do not know what fault I have committed against high or low. If there is good, I dare not conceal it; if there is evil, I dare not pardon it. Judgment resides with the mind of God. If the myriad regions have any fault, may it rest upon my person; but if I have any fault, may it not extend to the myriad regions.'" This shows that, though T'ang was honored as the Son of Heaven and possessed all the riches of the world, he did not hesitate to offer himself as a sacrifice in his prayers and entreaties to the Lord on High and the spirits. Such was the universality of T'ang, and the universality which Mo Tzu has been telling you about is patterned after that of T'ang.

This idea is expressed not only in the "Speech of T'ang" but in the odes of Chou as well. In the odes of Chou it says:

[3] A section of the *Book of Documents,* now lost.
[4] A section of the *Book of Documents,* now lost. Almost the same quotation is found at the beginning of Book XX of the Confucian *Analects.*

Broad, broad is the way of the king,
Neither partial nor partisan.
Fair, fair is the way of the king,
Neither partisan nor partial.

It is straight like an arrow,
Smooth like a whetstone.
The superior man treads it;
The small man looks upon it.[5]

So what I have been speaking about is no mere theory of action. In ancient times, when Kings Wen and Wu administered the government and assigned each person his just share, they rewarded the worthy and punished the wicked without showing any favoritism toward their own kin or brothers. Such was the universality of Kings Wen and Wu, and the universality which Mo Tzu has been telling you about is patterned after that of Wen and Wu. I cannot understand how the men of the world can hear about this doctrine of universality and still criticize it!

And yet the men of the world continue to criticize, saying, "If one takes no thought for what is beneficial or harmful to one's parents, how can one be called filial?"

Mo Tzu said: Let us examine for a moment the way in which a filial son plans for the welfare of his parents. When a filial son plans for his parents, does he wish others to love and benefit them, or does he wish others to hate and injure them? It stands to reason that he wishes others to love and benefit his parents. Now if I am a filial son, how do I go about accomplishing this? Do I first make it a point to love and benefit other men's parents, so that they in return will love

---

[5] The first four lines are now found, not in the *Book of Odes,* but in the *Hung fan* section of the *Book of Documents.* The last four lines are from the *Book of Odes, Hsiao ya* section, "Ta tung" (Mao text no. 203).

and benefit my parents? Or do I first make it a point to hate and injure other men's parents, so that they in return will love and benefit my parents? Obviously, I must first make it a point to love and benefit other men's parents, so that they in return will love and benefit my parents. So if all of us are to be filial sons, can we set about it any other way than by first making a point of loving and benefiting other men's parents? And are we to suppose that the filial sons of the world are all too stupid to be capable of doing what is right?

Let us examine further. Among the books of the former kings, in the "Greater Odes" of the *Book of Odes,* it says:

> There are no words that are not answered,
> No kindness that is not requited.
> Throw me a peach,
> I'll requite you a plum.[6]

The meaning is that one who loves will be loved by others, and one who hates will be hated by others. So I cannot understand how the men of the world can hear about this doctrine of universality and still criticize it!

Do they believe that it is too difficult to carry out? Yet there are much more difficult things that have been carried out. In the past King Ling of the state of Ching loved slender waists. During his reign, the people of Ching ate no more than one meal a day, until they were too weak to stand up without a cane, or to walk without leaning against the wall. Now reducing one's diet is a difficult thing to do, and yet people did it because it pleased King Ling. So within the space of a single generation the ways of the people can be

---

[6] The first two lines are from the poem "Yi" (Mao text no. 256), in the "Greater Odes" or *Ta ya* section of the *Book of Odes.* The last two lines, though not found in exactly this form, bear a close resemblance to lines in the poem "Mu-kua" (Mao text no. 64), in the *Kuo feng* or "Airs from the States" section of the *Odes.*

changed, for they will strive to ingratiate themselves with their superiors.

Again in the past King Kou-chien of Yüeh admired bravery and for three years trained his soldiers and subjects to be brave. But he was not sure whether they had understood the true meaning of bravery, and so he set fire to his warships and then sounded the drum to advance. The soldiers trampled each other down in their haste to go forward, and countless numbers of them perished in the fire and water. At that time, even though he ceased to drum them forward, they did not retreat. The soldiers of Yüeh were truly astonishing. Now consigning one's body to the flames is a difficult thing to do, and yet they did it because it pleased the king of Yüeh. So within the space of a single generation the ways of the people can be changed, for they will strive to ingratiate themselves with their superiors.

Duke Wen of Chin liked coarse clothing, and so during his reign the men of the state of Chin wore robes of coarse cloth, wraps of sheepskin, hats of plain silk, and big rough shoes, whether they were appearing before the duke in the inner chamber or walking about in the outer halls of the court. Now bringing oneself to wear coarse clothing is a difficult thing to do, and yet people did it because it pleased Duke Wen. So within the space of a single generation the ways of the people can be changed, for they will strive to ingratiate themselves with their superiors.

To reduce one's diet, consign one's body to the flames, or wear coarse clothing are among the most difficult things in the world to do. And yet people will do them because they know their superiors will be pleased. So within the space of a single generation the ways of the people can be changed.

Why? Because they will strive to ingratiate themselves with their superiors.

Now universal love and mutual benefit are both profitable and easy beyond all measure. The only trouble, as I see it, is that no ruler takes any delight in them. If the rulers really delighted in them, promoted them with rewards and praise, and prevented neglect of them by punishments, then I believe that people would turn to universal love and mutual benefit as naturally as fire turns upward or water turns downward, and nothing in the world could stop them.

The principle of universality is the way of the sage kings, the means of bringing safety to the rulers and officials and of assuring ample food and clothing to the people. Therefore the superior man can do no better than to examine it carefully and strive to put it into practice. If he does, then as a ruler he will be generous, as a subject loyal, as a father kind, as a son filial, as an older brother comradely, and as a younger brother respectful. So if the superior man wishes to be a generous ruler, a loyal subject, a kind father, a filial son, a comradely older brother, and a respectful younger brother, he must put into practice this principle of universality. It is the way of the sage kings and a great benefit to the people.

AGAINST OFFENSIVE WARFARE
PART I

(SECTION 17)

If a man enters an orchard and steals the peaches and plums, everyone who hears about it will condemn him, and if those above who administer the government catch him they will punish him. Why? Because he injures others to benefit himself. When it comes to carrying off dogs, swine, chickens, and piglings, the deed is even more unrighteous than entering an orchard to steal peaches and plums. Why? Because the loss to others is greater. It shows a greater lack of benevolence and is a more serious crime. When it comes to breaking into another man's stable and seizing his horses and cows, the deed is even more unrighteous than carrying off dogs, swine, chickens, and piglings. Why? Because the loss to others is greater, and if the loss is greater, it shows a greater lack of benevolence and is a more serious crime. And when it comes to murdering an innocent man, stripping him of his clothing, and appropriating his spear and sword, the deed is even more unrighteous than breaking into a stable and seizing someone's horses and cows. Why? Because the injury to others is even greater, and if the injury is greater, it shows a greater lack of benevolence and is a more serious crime.

Now all the gentlemen in the world know enough to condemn such acts and brand them as unrighteous. And yet when it comes to the even greater unrighteousness of offensive warfare against other states, they do not know enough to condemn it. On the contrary, they praise it and call it righteous. Is this what it means to know the difference between righteousness and unrighteousness?

If someone kills one man, he is condemned as unrighteous and must pay for his crime with his own life. According to this reasoning, if someone kills ten men, then he is ten times as unrighteous and should pay for his crime with ten lives, or if he kills a hundred men he is a hundred times as unrighteous and should pay for his crime with a hundred lives.

Now all the gentlemen in the world know enough to condemn such crimes and brand them as unrighteous. And yet when it comes to the even greater unrighteousness of offensive warfare against other states, they do not know enough to condemn it. On the contrary, they praise it and call it righteous. Truly they do not know what unrighteousness is. So they make a record of their wars to be handed down to posterity. If they knew that such wars were unrighteous, then what reason would they have for making a record of their unrighteous deeds to be handed down to posterity?

Now if there were a man who, on seeing a little bit of black, called it black but, on seeing a lot of black, called it white, we would conclude that he could not tell the difference between black and white. Or if there were a man who, on tasting a little bit of bitterness, called it bitter but, on tasting a lot, called it sweet, we would conclude that he could not distinguish between bitter and sweet. Now when a great wrong is committed and a state is attacked, men do not know enough to condemn it, but on the contrary praise it and call it righteous. Is this what it means to be able to distinguish between righteousness and unrighteousness? So we know that the gentlemen of the world are confused about the distinction between righteousness and unrighteousness.

PART III

Mo Tzu said: When the people of the world praise something as good, what is their reason? Do they praise it because it brings benefit to Heaven on high, to the spirits in the middle realm, and to mankind below? Or do they praise it because it fails to bring benefit to Heaven on high, to the spirits in the middle realm, and to mankind below? Even the stupidest man will reply that it is praised because it brings benefit to Heaven on high, to the spirits in the middle realm, and to mankind below.

Everyone agrees that the ways of the sage kings constitute a standard of righteousness. Yet many of the feudal lords of today continue to attack and annex their neighboring states. They claim they are honoring righteousness, but they fail to examine the truth of the matter. They are like blind men, who talk about black and white in the same way as ordinary men, but in practice cannot distinguish between them. Can this be called real discrimination?

Therefore when the wise men of ancient times planned for the welfare of the world, they were careful to consider and accord with what is right, and only then did they act. So there was no uncertainty in their movements, and they achieved speedy success and certain realization of their desires. To accord with what benefits Heaven, the spirits, and the common people—this is the way of the wise man.

Similarly, when the benevolent men of ancient times ruled the world, they strove for amicable relations among the large states, united the world in harmony, brought together all within the four seas, and led the people to serve and honor the Lord on High, the sacred mountains and rivers, and the spirits. Many were the benefits they brought to mankind, and great was their success. Therefore Heaven rewarded them, the spirits enriched them, and men praised them. They were honored with the rank of Son of Heaven, enriched with the possession of the world, and their names formed a triad with those of Heaven and earth, enduring to this day. Such, then, are the way of the wise man and the means by which the former kings held possession of the world.

But the rulers and feudal lords of today are not like this. They all set about to examine the relative merits of their soldiers, who are their teeth and claws, arrange their boat and chariot forces, and then, clad in strong armor and bearing sharp weapons, they set off to attack some innocent state. As soon as they enter the borders of the state, they begin cutting down the grain crops, felling trees, razing walls and fortifications, filling up moats and ponds, slaughtering the sacrificial animals, firing the ancestral temples of the state, massacring its subjects, trampling down its aged and weak, and carrying off its vessels and treasures. The soldiers are urged forward into battle by being told, "To die in the cause of duty is the highest honor, to kill a large number of the enemy is the next highest, and to be wounded is next. But as for breaking ranks and fleeing in defeat—the penalty for that is death without hope of pardon!" So the soldiers are filled with fear.

Now to seize a state and overthrow its army, massacre its subjects, and undo the labors of the sages—is this intended to benefit Heaven? Yet it is the people of Heaven who are gathered together to attack a city of Heaven.[1] So they are

---

[1] I.e., all men are the people of Heaven and all cities are its cities.

massacring the subjects of Heaven, driving out the spirits of their ancestors, overthrowing their altars of the soil and grain, and slaughtering their sacrificial animals. This brings no benefit to Heaven on high. Is it intended then to benefit the spirits? But to murder men is to wipe out the caretakers of the spirits, to cause the spirits of the former kings to suffer neglect, to oppress the subjects of the state and scatter its people. This brings no benefit to the spirits in the middle realm. Is it intended then to benefit mankind? But murdering men is a paltry way to benefit them indeed, and when we calculate the expenditures for such warfare we find that they have crippled the basis of the nation's livelihood and exhausted the resources of the people to an incalculable degree. This brings no benefit to mankind below.

Now when the armies fail to gain any advantage over each other, they say, "If our generals are not brave, our officers not spirited, our weapons not sharp, our ranks not well drilled, our force not large, our soldiers not in harmony, our authority not firm, our sieges not sustained, our assaults not swift, our control over the people not strict, and our hearts not hardened, then our allies among the other feudal lords will begin to doubt us, and if our allies begin to doubt us, then the enemy will have time to lay his plans and fulfill his desires.[2] But even if all these conditions are met before one sets out to war, the state will still lose its fighting men and the common people will be forced to abandon their occupations. Let us examine the reason for this.

When a state which delights in aggressive warfare raises an army, it must have several hundred high officers, several thousand regular officers, and a hundred thousand soldiers, before it can set out. The time required for the expedition will

[2] Reading *ying* instead of *lei*.

be several years at the longest, several months at the least. During that time the leaders will have no time to attend to affairs of government, the officials no time to manage their departments of state, the farmers no time to sow or reap, the women no time to spin or weave. So in this case too the state will lose its fighting men and the common people will be forced to abandon their occupations. Moreover, there will be the damage and depreciation to the horses and chariots to consider, while if one fifth of the tents and hangings, army supplies, and weapons can be salvaged from the campaign, the state will be lucky. In addition, a countless number of men will desert or become lost along the way, or will die and end tumbled in a ditch due to the starvation, cold, and sickness caused by the length of the journey or the fact that supplies do not arrive in time.[3]

Such is the injury which warfare inflicts upon men, the harm it brings to the world. And yet the rulers and officials delight in carrying out such expeditions. In effect they are taking delight in the injury and extermination of the people of the world. Are they not perverse?

At present the states in the world which are fondest of warfare are Ch'i, Chin, Ch'u, and Yüeh. If these four states were in a position to order the rest of the world about, they could easily increase their present populations by tenfold and still have land left over to feed even more. This is because they have too few people and an excess of land. And yet now they go to war with each other over land and succeed only in doing further injury to each other's people. This is simply to destroy what one does not have enough of for the sake of what one already has in excess!

[3] The text of this paragraph and the preceding one is in poor condition and the translation at numerous points is highly tentative.

Now these rulers who delight in offensive warfare attempt to put a pleasing façade upon their doctrines and criticize Mo Tzu, saying, "Do you claim that offensive warfare is an unrighteous and unprofitable thing? In ancient times Yü launched an expedition against the ruler of the Miao, T'ang attacked Chieh, and King Wu attacked Chou, and yet all three are regarded as sage kings. Why is this?"

Mo Tzu said: You have failed to examine the terminology which I employ and do not understand the reasoning behind it. What these men did was not to "attack" but to "punish."

In ancient times the three Miao tribes were in great disorder and Heaven decreed their destruction. The sun came out at night and for three days it rained blood. A dragon appeared in the ancestral temple and dogs howled in the market place. Ice formed in summertime, the earth split open until springs gushed forth, the five grains grew all deformed, and the people were filled with a great terror. Kao Yang gave the command in the Dark Palace, and Yü in person grasped the jade staff of authority and set out to subdue the ruler of the Miao. Amidst the din of thunder and lightning, a spirit with the face of a man and the body of a bird came bearing a jade baton to wait upon Yü. The general of the Miao was felled by an arrow, and the Miao army thrown into great confusion. After this their power waned. When Yü had conquered the three Miao, he marked off the mountains and rivers, separated those things which pertained to above and below, and clearly regulated the four extremities of the world, so that neither spirits nor people committed any offense, and all the world was at peace. This was how Lü launched an expedition against the ruler of the Miao.[4]

[4] The text of this and the two succeeding paragraphs is in poor condition and requires considerable emendation before it will yield any sense. We

In the case of King Chieh of Hsia, Heaven likewise sent down its direst command. Sun and moon failed to appear at the proper time, hot weather and cold mingled in confusion, and the five grains were seared and died. Spirits wailed throughout the land and cranes shrieked for more than ten nights. Heaven gave its command to T'ang in the Piao Palace, ordering him to take over the solemn mandate from the Hsia, for the Hsia had fallen into grave disorder.[5] Only then did T'ang dare to lead forth his troops in obedience to the command and advance toward the border of Hsia, and God caused the city of Hsia to be secretly overthrown.[6] After a while a spirit appeared and reported to T'ang: "The virtue of the Hsia is in great disorder. Go and attack it, and I will surely cause you to win victory over it, for I have already received the command from Heaven." Then Heaven ordered Chu-jung to send down fire on the northwest corner of the city of Hsia, and T'ang, leading the army of Chieh, conquered it. Then he summoned all the nobles to Po and made clear to them the command of Heaven, sending word of it to the four quarters, and none of the feudal lords in the world failed to do obeisance to him. This was how T'ang punished Chieh.

In the case of King Chou of Shang, Heaven would not sanction his power. His sacrifices were untimely; for ten days and ten nights it rained earth at Po, and the nine cauldrons moved about. Phantom women came out after dark and ghosts wailed at night. A woman turned into a man, flesh rained down from Heaven, and brambles grew on the state roads.

---

have little information concerning the various legends to which Mo Tzu here refers, and what we have is mostly from later writers, confused and contradictory.

[5] The seventeen characters which follow at this point seem to be a ditto-graph of the speech of the spirit, and have been omitted in translation.

[6] The meaning of the last part of the sentence is very doubtful.

And yet the king continued to behave in an even more willful and abandoned way. A red bird holding in its beak a baton of jade alighted at the altar of the Chou state in the city of Ch'i and proclaimed: "Heaven orders King Wen of Chou to attack Yin [i.e., Shang] [7] and take possession of its state." T'ai-tien journeyed to pay his respects to the Chou ruler, the river cast up its chart, and the land brought forth the "riding-yellow" beast.[8] King Wu ascended the throne, and in a dream he saw three spirits who said to him: "We have already drowned Chou of Shang in the power of wine. Go and attack him, and we will surely cause you to win victory over him!" So King Wu went and attacked him, and replaced the state of Shang with that of Chou, and Heaven presented King Wu with the yellow bird pennant. After King Wu had conquered the Shang dynasty and received the gifts bestowed by God, he assigned guardians to the various spirits, instituted sacrifices to Chou's ancestors, the former kings of Shang, and opened up communications with the barbarians of the four quarters, so that there was no one in the world who did not pay him allegiance. This was how he carried on the labors of T'ang. Thus, if we examine the cases of these three sage kings, we will see that what they did was not to "attack" but to "punish."

But still those rulers who delight in offensive warfare attempt to put a pleasing façade upon their doctrines and criticize Mo Tzu, saying, "Do you claim that offensive warfare is an unrighteous and unprofitable thing? In ancient times Hsiung-li, the founder of the state of Ch'u, was first enfeoffed in the region of Mount Sui; Yi-k'uei, a descendant of Hsiung-

---

[7] Or perhaps the text should be emended to read "replace Yin."

[8] A mythical beast, said to resemble a fox and to have two horns growing out of its back.

ch'ü, was made ruler of the state of Yüeh; while T'ang-shu and Lü Shang were given possession of the states of Chin and Ch'i respectively. All of these states originally covered an area of no more than a few hundred *li* square, and yet by annexing their neighbors they have succeeded in dividing up the world among the four of them. How do you explain this?"

Mo Tzu said: You have failed to examine the terminology I employ and do not understand the reasoning behind it. In ancient times the Son of Heaven enfeoffed over ten thousand feudal lords. And yet now, because of the annexation of one state by another, these ten thousand domains have all disappeared and only the four remain.[9] But it is rather like the case of a doctor who administers medicine to over ten thousand patients but succeeds in curing only four. He cannot be said to be a very skilled physician.

Yet these rulers who delight in offensive warfare attempt once more to put a pleasing façade upon their doctrines, saying, "It is not that we have any lack of gold and jewels, courtiers and waiting women, or land. It is only that we wish to establish a reputation for righteousness in the world and attract the other rulers to our virtue!"

Mo Tzu said: If you were really able to establish a reputation for righteousness in the world and attract the other rulers by your virtue, then it would be no time at all before the whole world had submitted to you, for the world has for a long time been plagued by warfare and is as weary as a little boy who has spent the day playing horse. Now if only there

---

[9] This is rather misleading. There were over a dozen more or less independent states in China in Mo Tzu's time, though the four he mentions, Ch'i, Chin, Ch'u, and Yüeh, seem to have been the most powerful. The state of Ch'in, which eventually conquered the others and united China, was at this time undergoing a period of internal disorder and hence Mo Tzu does not list it among the great powers.

were someone who would conduct his diplomatic affairs in good faith and would think first of all how to benefit the other feudal lords; who, when a large state committed some unrighteous act, would feel concerned along with others; who, when a large state attacked a small one, would go to the rescue of the small state along with others; who, when the walls and fortifications of the smaller state were in poor condition, would see to it that they were repaired; who, when the smaller state's supplies of cloth and grain were exhausted, would supply more; who, when the smaller state's funds were insufficient, would share his own—if one were to conduct his relations with the large states in this manner, then the rulers of the smaller states would be pleased. If others struggle while one is at ease, then one's own military position will become stronger. If one is merciful and generous, substituting affluence for want, then the people will surely be won over. If one substitutes good government in one's own state for offensive warfare, then one will achieve manifold success. If one weighs the expenditures of one's own army and compares them with the ruinous expenditures of the other feudal lords, one will see that one has gained rich benefits. If one conducts one's affairs in accordance with what is correct, acts in the name of righteousness, strives for lenience in ruling one's subjects and good faith in dealing with one's army, and thus sets an example for the armies of the other feudal lords, then one will have no enemy under heaven and will bring incalculable benefit to the world.

This is what benefits the world, and if the rulers and officials do not know enough to make use of it, then they cannot be said to understand the most important way of benefiting the world.

Therefore Mo Tzu said: If the rulers and officials and gentlemen of the world sincerely desire to promote what is beneficial to the world and to eliminate what is harmful, they should realize that offensive warfare is in fact a great harm to the world. If they wish to practice benevolence and righteousness and become superior men; if they wish to act in accordance with the way of the sage kings and benefit the people of China, they should not fail to examine what I have said in my condemnation of offensive warfare.

MODERATION IN EXPENDITURE
PART I

(SECTION 20)

When a sage governs a state, the benefits to the state **are** doubled; when he governs the world, the benefits to the world are doubled. The doubling is not accomplished by acquiring territory outside, but by eliminating needless expenditures within the state itself. In this way the benefits can be doubled. When the sage administers the government, in issuing orders, beginning enterprises, employing the people, or expending wealth, he does not do anything that is not in some way useful. Therefore wealth is not wasted, the strength of the people is not taxed, and yet many benefits are procured.

What is the purpose of making clothing? To keep out the cold in winter and the heat in summer. Therefore the way to make clothing is to design something that will provide warmth in winter and coolness in summer. Whatever is merely decorative and does not contribute to these ends should be avoided.

What is the purpose of building houses? To keep out the wind and cold in winter and the heat and rain in summer, and to provide protection against thieves. Whatever is merely decorative and does not contribute to these ends should be avoided.

What is the purpose of armor, shields, and the various kinds of weapons? To provide protection against rebels and bandits. When faced with rebels and bandits, if one has armor, shield, and weapons, one can overcome them, but if not, one is helpless. Therefore the sages made armor, shields, and weapons. One tries to make them as light, sharp, durable, and difficult to break as possible. What is merely decorative and does not contribute to these ends should be avoided.

What is the purpose of making boats and carts? In the case of carts it is to provide a means of getting about on land and in the case of boats to provide a means of traveling on rivers, so that all areas may enjoy the benefits of communication with each other. In making boats and carts, one strives for lightness and convenience. What is merely decorative and does not contribute to these ends should be avoided.

In making these five things, nothing is done that does not contribute to their usefulness. Therefore wealth is not wasted, the strength of the people is not taxed, and yet many benefits are procured.

If one can persuade the rulers to give up their passion for collecting jewels, birds, beasts, dogs, and horses, and to increase the amount of clothing, houses, armor, shields, weapons, boats, and carts, then it is easy enough to double the number of these articles.

What, then, is it difficult to double the number of? It is difficult to double the number of people. And yet it can be done.

In ancient times, the sage kings made a law saying: "No man of twenty shall dare to be without a family; no woman of fifteen shall dare to be without a husband." Such was the law of the sage kings.[1] But since the sage kings passed away, the people have taken to following their own desires. Those who want to have a family early in some cases marry at twenty;

[1] So says Mo Tzu. But a Confucian work, the *Chou li* or *Rites of Chou,* which claims to represent the practices of the early Chou, under *mei shih* (the match-maker), prescribes the marriage age as thirty for men and twenty for women.

those who want to have a family late in some cases marry at forty. The average marrying age is therefore ten years later than that prescribed by the law of the sage kings. Since families usually have one child in three years, then by marrying earlier they could have had two or three children during those ten years. But can one double the population without causing the people to marry early? Certainly not!

There are many ways in which the rulers of the world today actually cause their populations to decrease. They work the people until they are weary and exact heavy taxes from them, so that the wealth of the people is exhausted and countless numbers of them die of cold and starvation. Moreover, the rulers insist upon raising armies and setting off to attack neighboring states, the expeditions lasting sometimes as long as three years, or at the shortest three months. Thus men and women are separated for long periods of time, and this serves in effect to diminish the population. Countless numbers die of insecure living conditions, irregular food, and sickness, while countless more are killed in ambushes, fire attacks, assaults on cities, and battles in the open field. Does it not seem, then, that the rulers of today are deliberately inventing ways of diminishing the population? These did not exist when the sages administered their rule. When they administered their rule, they invented ways of increasing the population, did they not?

Therefore Mo Tzu said: To do away with needless expenditure is the way of the sage kings and the source of great benefit to the world.

MODERATION IN FUNERALS
PART III

(SECTION 25)

Mo Tzu said: The benevolent man in planning for the welfare of the empire is no different from a filial son planning for the welfare of his parents, is he? Now when a filial son plans for the welfare of his parents, what is it he aims at? If his parents are poor, he seeks to enrich them; if the members of the family are few, he seeks to increase their number; if the family is in disorder, he seeks to bring it to order. In his efforts he may in time find his strength prove insufficient, his wealth inadequate, and his wisdom wanting. And yet so long as he has unused strength, untried schemes, and unrealized prospects for benefit, he dares not cease working for the welfare of his parents. It is by seeking these three aims that the filial son plans for the welfare of his parents. The same is true of the benevolent man planning for the welfare of the world. If the people of the world are poor, he seeks to enrich them; if they are few, he seeks to increase their number; and if they are in disorder, he seeks to bring them to order. In his efforts he may in time find his strength prove insufficient, his wealth inadequate, and his wisdom wanting. And yet so long as he has unused strength, untried schemes, and unrealized prospects for benefit, he dares not cease working for the welfare of the world. It is by seeking these three aims that the benevolent man plans for the welfare of the world.

Now that the sage kings of the Three Dynasties of antiquity have passed away and the world has forgotten their principles, there are some gentlemen of later ages who maintain that elaborate funerals and lengthy mourning are manifestations of benevolence and righteousness and the duty of a filial son, while there are others who maintain that elaborate funerals and lengthy mourning are contrary to benevolence and righteousness and should not be practiced by filial sons. The proponents of these two views are directly opposed in their words and actions, and yet both sides claim that they are following the way handed down from antiquity by Yao, Shun, Yü, T'ang, Wen, and Wu. Since their words and actions are contradictory, people are in doubt as to which to follow. If people are in doubt as to which to follow, let us try examining the government of the state and its people and see to what degree elaborate funerals and lengthy mourning contribute to the three aims of the benevolent man mentioned above.

In my opinion, if by following the principles and adopting the instructions of those who advocate elaborate funerals and lengthy mourning one can actually enrich the poor, increase the population, and bring stability and order to the state, then such principles are in accordance with benevolence and righteousness and are the duty of a filial son. Those who lay plans for the state cannot but recommend them, and the benevolent man seeking to promote what is beneficial to the world cannot but adopt them and cause the people to praise and follow them all their lives. If, on the other hand, by following the principles and adopting the instructions of those who advocate elaborate funerals and lengthy mourning one cannot actually enrich the poor, increase the population, and bring stability and order to the nation, then such principles are not in accordance with benevolence and righteousness and are not the duty of a filial son. In that case those who lay plans for the state cannot but oppose them, and the benevolent man seeking to eliminate what is harmful to the world cannot but discard them and cause the people to condemn and shun them all their lives. For it has never happened that, by promoting what is beneficial to the world and eliminating what is harmful, one has failed to bring order to the states and people of the world. How do we know that this is so?

There are still many gentlemen in the world today who are in doubt as to whether elaborate funerals and lengthy mourning are actually right or wrong, beneficial or harmful. Therefore Mo Tzu said: Let us try examining the matter. If we follow the rules of those who advocate elaborate funerals and lengthy mourning and apply them in the state, then, we are told, the funeral of a king or high minister will require several inner and outer coffins, a deep grave, numerous grave clothes, a large amount of embroidery for decorating the coffins, and a large grave mound. If the family of the deceased happen to be humble commoners the wealth of the family will be exhausted, and if they are feudal lords their treasuries will be emptied. After the above articles have been supplied, one still needs gold, jewels, and pearls to adorn the corpse, and bundles of silk, carriages, and horses to inter in the grave. In addition there must be draperies and hangings, tripods, baskets, tables, mats, vessels, basins, spears, swords, feather banners, and articles of ivory and hide to bury with the dead before the requirements are fulfilled. And as to those who are chosen to accompany the dead, in the case of a Son of Heaven anywhere from several ten to several hundred persons will be sacrificed, while in the case of generals or high ministers the number will be from several to several tens.

And what are the rules to be observed by the mourner? We

are told that he must wail and cry in a sobbing voice at irregular intervals, wearing hemp mourning garments and with tears running down his face. He must live in a mourning hut, sleep on a straw mat, and use a clod of earth for a pillow. In addition he is urged not to eat so as to appear starved, to wear thin clothes so as to appear cold, to acquire a lean and sickly look and a dark complexion. His ears and eyes are to appear dull, his hands and feet lacking in strength, as though he had lost the use of them. And in the case of higher officials we are told that during a period of mourning they should be unable to rise without support or to walk without a cane. And all this is to last for three years.[1]

Now if the rulers and high officials are to adopt these practices, they cannot appear at court early and retire late, attend to the five ministries and six bureaus, encourage farming and forestry, and fill the granaries. If the farmers are to adopt these practices, they cannot leave their homes early and return late, planting their fields and cultivating their crops. If the artisans are to adopt these practices, they cannot construct boats and carts and fashion dishes and utensils, while if women are to adopt these practices they cannot devote themselves day and night to spinning and weaving.

Thus we see that in elaborate funerals much wealth is buried, while lengthy mourning prevents people from going about their activities for long periods of time. If the wealth and goods that have already been produced are to be bundled

---

[1] Not three whole years, but into the third year, i.e., twenty-five months. On the whole, Mo Tzu's description of elaborate funerals and mourning practices follows what was prescribed by the Confucians, though the latter stressed that mourning practices were never to be carried to the point where they endangered the health of the mourner. It should be noted, however, that the Confucians never advocated the ancient and grisly custom of human sacrifice—the so-called "following in death" which Mo Tzu mentions—but on the contrary took every opportunity to denounce it.

p and buried in the ground, and the means of future produc-
on are to be prohibited for long periods of time, and one still
opes in this way to enrich the state, then it is like prohibiting
planting and still hoping for a harvest. One could never
acquire wealth that way!

Thus if one hopes to enrich the state, this is obviously not
the way to do it. But if one hopes to increase the population,
then are elaborate funerals and lengthy mourning perhaps
of benefit? Again we find that the answer is no.

Now suppose one follows the rules of those who advocate
elaborate funerals and lengthy mourning and applies them in
government. We are told that one should mourn three years
on the death of a ruler, three years on the death of a parent,
three years for a wife or eldest son, one year for paternal
uncles, brothers, and younger sons, five months for other close
relatives, and several months for aunts, sisters, and cousins on
the maternal side. There are rules requiring one to appear
emaciated, to acquire a lean and sickly look, a dark complexion,
ears and eyes that are dull, hands and feet that are lacking in
strength and useless. And in the case of higher officials we
are told that they should be unable to rise without support or
to walk without a cane. And all of this in most cases is to last
three years. Yet if these practices are adopted and people really
are reduced to a starved condition, then the common people
will be unable to bear the cold in winter or the heat in
summer, and countless numbers of them will sicken and die.
Moreover, the relations between men and women will in many
cases be disrupted. To hope in this way to increase the population is like ordering a man to fall upon his sword and wishing
him long life.

Thus if one hopes to increase the population, this is obviously not the way to do it. But if one hopes to bring order to

the government, then are elaborate funerals and lengthy mourning perhaps of benefit? Again we find that the answer is no.

If one follows the rules of those who advocate elaborate funerals and lengthy mourning and applies them in government, then the state will become poor, the people few, and the government disordered. For if one applies these rules, then those in superior positions will be unable to attend to affairs of government, while those in inferior positions will be unable to pursue their tasks. If those in superior positions do not attend to affairs of government, then disorder will result, and if those in inferior positions do not pursue their tasks, then there will not be enough food and clothing. And if there is not enough food and clothing, then the younger brother, seeking help from his older brother but receiving none, will feel no more love for his older brother but instead will come to hate him. Similarly, the son, seeking help from his father but receiving none, will become unfilial and will hate his father. And the minister, seeking help from his lord but receiving none, will become disloyal and will turn against his superior. Then evil and immoral people, with neither clothing to go abroad in nor food at home, will be stung by shame in their hearts and will give themselves up to uncontrollable evil and violence. Thus thieves and bandits increase in number and lawabiding persons grow few. If thieves and bandits increase in number and law-abiding persons grow few, and yet one seeks in this way to achieve order, it would be like ordering a man to turn around three times without showing his back to you.

If one hopes to achieve order, this is obviously not the way to do it. But if one hopes to prevent large states from attacking small ones, then are elaborate funerals and lengthy mourning perhaps of some use? Again we find that the answer is no.

Now that the sage kings of antiquity have passed away and the world has forgotten their principles, the feudal lords rely upon force of arms to attack each other. In the south are the kings of Ch'u and Yüeh, and in the north the lords of Ch'i and Chin, all of whom drill and discipline their soldiers, attack and annex their neighbors, and seek to rule the world. Only one thing will deter a large state from attacking a small one, and that is for the small state to have a plentiful supply of provisions, walls and fortifications in good repair, and superiors and subordinates who work in harmony. In that case the large states will have no desire to attack.

Now if one follows the rules of those who advocate elaborate funerals and lengthy mourning, and applies them in government, then the state will become poor, the people few, and the government disordered. If the state is poor, it cannot store up plentiful supplies of provisions. If the people are few, there will not be enough men to keep the fortifications and moats in repair. And if the government is disordered, then the state will be unable to win victory abroad or defend its position at home.

Thus, if one hopes to prevent large states from attacking small ones, this is obviously not the way to do it. But if one hopes to win blessing from the Lord on High and the spirits, then are elaborate funerals and lengthy mourrning perhaps of some use? Again the answer is no.

Now if one follows the rules of those who advocate elaborate funerals and lengthy mourning, and applies them in government, then the state will become poor, the people few, and the government disordered. If the state is poor, then its offerings of millet and wine will not be of the required purity. If the people are few, there will not be enough of them to serve the Lord on High and the spirits. And if the government is disordered, then the sacrifices will not be conducted at the proper times or in the proper fashion. Now if one conducts the government in this way, effectively preventing the proper worship of the Lord on High and the spirits, then the Lord on High and the spirits will look down from above and, considering how to deal with the people, will say to each other: "Is it better for us that these people exist or that they cease to exist? It makes no difference to us whether they exist or not!" Then the Lord on High and the spirits will send down chastisement for the people's faults and harsh punishment, and will abandon them. And they will have good reason for doing so, will they not?

Therefore the ancient sage kings prescribed the following rules for funerals and mourning: A coffin three inches thick is sufficient to bury a rotting body; three pieces of clothing are sufficient to cover a smelly corpse. In interring the coffin, it should not be placed deep enough to reach water, nor so near the surface as to allow the odor to escape. A grave mound three feet in height is large enough. After the dead one has been buried, the living shall engage in no prolonged mourning, but shall return speedily to their tasks, each doing whatever he is able to do and working for the benefit of others. Such were the rules of the sage kings.

Now those who advocate elaborate funerals and lengthy mourning say: "Although elaborate funerals and lengthy mourning cannot enrich the poor, increase the population, and insure stability and order, yet they represent the way of the sage kings."

Mo Tzu said: This is not so. In ancient times, when Yao

went north to instruct the eight Ti tribes, he died on the way and was buried on the north side of Mount Ch'iung. Three pieces of clothing wrapped his corpse, and the coffin was of a poor variety of wood and tied shut with vines. No wailing was done until after the coffin was interred. The grave was filled in, but no mound was constructed, and after the burial horses and oxen plodded over the ground the same as before.

When Shun went west to instruct the seven Jung tribes, he died on the way and was buried in the market place of Nan-chi. Three pieces of clothing wrapped his corpse, and the coffin was of a poor variety of wood and tied shut with vines. After the burial the people in the market walked over the spot the same as before.

When Yü went east to instruct the nine Yi tribes, he died on the way and was buried at Mount K'uai-chi. Three pieces of clothing wrapped his corpse, and the coffin was made of soft paulownia wood, three inches thick, and tied shut with vines. The coffin was not tightly bound shut, nor was a large pit dug. The grave was not deep enough to strike water, but not so shallow as to allow the odor to escape. After the burial the loose earth was gathered together on top to form a grave mound three feet in size, and this was considered sufficient.

So if we examine the case of these three sage kings, we can see that elaborate funerals and lengthy mourning do not in fact represent the way of the sage kings. These three kings were honored with the position of Son of Heaven and possessed the riches of the whole world. Surely they did not choose to be buried in this way because they were concerned about the expenditure!

But the burials of the rulers and officials of today are very different from this. They must have outer and inner coffins, three layers of embroidered hide, jades and jewels; and when these have been provided, they still require spears, swords, tripods, baskets, vessels, basins, embroideries, silks, countless horse bridles, carriages, horses, waiting women, and musicians. On top of this they demand roads and approaches to the grave going this way and that, and a mound as round and high as a hill.[2] All of this interferes with the daily labors of the people and wastes their wealth to an incalculable degree. Such is the uselessness of elaborate burials!

Therefore Mo Tzu said: I have already stated above that if, by following the rules and using the plans of those who advocate elaborate funerals and lengthy mourning, one can actually enrich the poor, increase the population, and bring stability and order to the government, then such principles must be in accordance with benevolence and righteousness and be the duty of a filial son. In that case those who lay plans for the state cannot but recommend them. But if, by following the rules and using the plans of those who advocate elaborate funerals and lengthy mourning, one cannot actually enrich the poor, increase the population, and bring stability and order to the government, then such principles are not in accordance with benevolence and righteousness and are not the duty of a filial son. In that case those who lay plans for the state cannot but condemn them. Therefore if one seeks to enrich the state by adopting such practices, he will only bring greater poverty; if he seeks to increase the population, he will only decrease it further; if he seeks to bring about order in government, he will only achieve greater disorder; if he seeks thereby to prevent large states from attacking small ones, he will have no hope of success; and if he seeks for blessing from

[2] The text of this passage is doubtful in several places, particularly the mention of "countless horse bridles," which should perhaps be emended to read "six carriage bells."

the Lord on High and the spirits, he will obtain only misfortune. If we examine the ways of the sage kings Yao, Shun, Yü, T'ang, Wen, and Wu, we find that they were the direct opposite of such practices. But if we examine the practices of the evil kings Chieh, Chou, Yu, and Li, we find that they accord exactly with these. From this we can see that elaborate funerals and lengthy mourning were not the way of the sage kings.

Now those who advocate elaborate funerals and lengthy mourning say: "If elaborate funerals and lengthy mourning are in fact not the way of the sage kings, then why do the gentlemen of China continue to practice them and not give them up? Why do they carry them out and not abandon them?"

Mo Tzu said: This is because they confuse what is habitual with what is proper, and what is customary with what is right. In ancient times east of the state of Yüeh lived the people of the land of K'ai-shu. When their first son was born, they cut him up and ate him, saying that this would be beneficial to the next son. When their fathers died, they loaded their mothers on their backs, carried them off and abandoned them, saying, "One can't live in the same house with the wife of a ghost!" These were regarded by the superiors as rules of government and by the people as accepted procedure. They continued to practice these customs and did not give them up, carried them out and did not abandon them. And yet can we actually say that they represent the way of benevolence and righteousness? This is what it means to accept what is habitual as proper, and what is customary as right.

South of Ch'u live the people of the land of Yen. When their parents die, they scrape the flesh off the dead person's bones and throw it away. After that they bury the bones, and thus consider that they have fulfilled their duty as filial sons.

West of Ch'in live the people of the land of Yi-ch'ü. When their parents die, they gather together brushwood and burn the bodies, and when the smoke rises up they say that the dead have "ascended far off." After this they feel that they have fulfilled their duty as filial sons. In these lands such customs are regarded by the superiors as rules of government, and by the people as accepted procedure. They continue to practice them and do not give them up, carry them out and do not abandon them. And yet can we actually say that they represent the way of benevolence and righteousness? This is what it means to accept what is habitual as proper, and what is customary as right.

If we examine the practices of these three lands, we find them too casual and heartless, while if we examine those of the gentlemen of China, we find them too elaborate. Some practices being too elaborate and others too casual, we must seek for moderation in the matter of funerals and burials. Food and clothing are the greatest benefit to the living, and yet they must be used with moderation. Since funerals and burials are the greatest benefit to the dead, how then can we fail to exercise moderation in their case as well?

Therefore Mo Tzu prescribes the following rules for funerals and burials: a coffin three inches thick is sufficient to bury rotting bones; three pieces of clothing are sufficient to cover rotting flesh. The hole in the ground should not be deep enough to reach dampness, nor so shallow that the gases escape above ground. A mound sufficiently large to mark the spot is all that is needed. Mourners may weep going to and from the burial, but after that they should devote themselves to making a living. Sacrifices should be carried out at appropriate times in order to fulfill one's filial duty to parents. Thus in this way the rules of Mo Tzu neglect the benefits of neither the living nor the dead.

So Mo Tzu said: If the officials and gentlemen of the world today sincerely desire to practice benevolence and righteousness and become superior men, if they wish to act in accordance with the way of the sage kings and to benefit the people of China, they ought to adopt moderation in funerals as a principle of government. They should not fail to examine the matter.

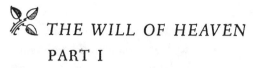

THE WILL OF HEAVEN
PART I
(SECTION 26)

Mo Tzu said: The gentlemen of the world today understand small matters but not large ones. How do we know this? We know it from the way they conduct themselves at home. If at home a man commits some offense against the head of the family, he may still run away and hide at a neighbor's house. And yet his parents, brothers, and friends will all join in warning and admonishing him, saying, "You must be more cautious! You must be more circumspect! When you are living at home, how can it be right for you to offend the head of the family?"

This is true not only of a man who lives at home, but of a man who lives in a state as well. If a man living in a state commits some offense against the ruler of the state, he may still run away and hide in a neighboring state. And yet his parents, brothers, and friends will all join in warning and admonishing him, saying, "You must be more cautious! You must be more circumspect! How can you live in a state and still consider it right to offend the ruler of the state?"

If people warn and admonish a man this sternly when he still has some place to run away to and hide, how much more sternly should they feel obliged to warn and admonish him if there is no place for him to run away and hide. There is a saying that goes: "If you commit a crime here in the broad daylight, where will you run and hide?" There is no place to run and hide, for Heaven will spy you out clearly even in the forest, the valley, or the dark and distant place where no one lives! And yet with regard to Heaven the gentlemen of the world for some reason do not know enough to warn and admonish each other. Thus I know that the gentlemen of the world understand small matters but not large ones.

Now what does Heaven desire and what does it hate? Heaven desires righteousness and hates unrighteousness. Thus if I lead the people of the world to devote themselves to righteousness, then I am doing what Heaven desires. If I do what Heaven desires, then Heaven will do what I desire. Now what do I desire and what do I hate? I desire good fortune and prosperity and hate misfortune and calamity. If I do not do what Heaven desires and instead do what Heaven does not desire, then I will be leading the people of the world to devote themselves to what will bring misfortune and calamity.

How do I know that Heaven desires righteousness and hates unrighteousness? In the world, where there is righteousness there is life; where there is no righteousness there is death. Where there is righteousness there is wealth; where there is no righteousness there is poverty. Where there is righteousness there is order; where there is no righteousness there is disorder. Now Heaven desires life and hates death, desires wealth and hates poverty, desires order and hates disorder. So I know that Heaven desires righteousness and hates unrighteousness.

Moreover, righteousness is what is right. Subordinates do not decide what is right for their superiors; it is the superiors who decide what is right for their subordinates. Therefore the common people devote their strength to carrying out their tasks, but they cannot decide for themselves what is right. There are gentlemen to do that for them. The gentlemen devote their strength to carrying out their tasks, but they cannot decide for themselves what is right. There are ministers and officials to do that for them. The ministers and officials devote their strength to carrying out their tasks, but they cannot decide for themselves what is right. There are the three high ministers and the feudal lords to do that for them. The three high ministers and the feudal lords devote their strength to managing the affairs of government, but they cannot decide for themselves what is right. There is the Son of Heaven to do that for them. But the Son of Heaven cannot decide for himself what is right. There is Heaven to decide that for him. The gentlemen of the world have no difficulty in perceiving that the Son of Heaven decides what is right for the three high ministers, the feudal lords, the gentlemen, and the common people. But the people of the world are unable to perceive that Heaven decides what is right for the Son of Heaven. Therefore Yü, T'ang, Wen, and Wu, the sage kings of the Three Dynasties of antiquity, wishing to make it clear to the people of the world that it is Heaven that decides what is right for the Son of Heaven, all without exception fed their sacrificial oxen and sheep, fattened their dogs and pigs, prepared clean offerings of millet and wine, and sacrificed to the Lord on High and the spirits in order to seek blessing and good fortune from Heaven. But I have never heard of Heaven seeking blessing and good fortune from the Son of Heaven! So I know that it is Heaven that decides what is right for the Son of Heaven.

The Son of Heaven is the most eminent person in the world and the richest in the world. He who desires riches and eminence must not fail to obey the will of Heaven. He who obeys the will of Heaven, loving all men universally and working for their benefit, will surely win reward. But he who disobeys the will of Heaven, showing partiality and hatred and working to injure others, will surely incur punishment. Who, then, were those who obeyed the will of Heaven and won reward, and who were those who disobeyed the will of Heaven and incurred punishment?

Mo Tzu said: Yü, T'ang, Wen, and Wu, the sage kings of the Three Dynasties of antiquity—they were the ones who obeyed the will of Heaven and won reward. Chieh, Chou, Yu, and Li, the evil kings of the Three Dynasties of antiquity—they were the ones who disobeyed the will of Heaven and incurred punishment.

How did Yü, T'ang, Wen, and Wu win reward? Mo Tzu said: Above they honored Heaven, in the middle realm they served the spirits, and below they loved men. Therefore the will of Heaven announced: "These men love all those I love and benefit all those I would benefit. They love men widely and benefit them greatly." Therefore Heaven caused them to be honored with the position of Son of Heaven, and enriched with the possession of the world. They were succeeded by their sons and grandsons for countless generations, and their goodness was praised throughout the world. Even today people praise them, calling them sage kings.

How did Chieh, Chou, Yu, and Li incur punishment? Mo Tzu said: Above they blasphemed against Heaven, in the middle realm they blasphemed against the spirits, and below they did harm to men. Therefore the will of Heaven announced: "These men show discrimination and hatred against those I love, and do harm to those I would benefit. They hate men widely and harm men greatly!" Therefore Heaven caused them to die before their time and to perish in a single generation, and even today people condemn them, calling them evil kings.

How do we know that Heaven loves the people of the

world? Because it enlightens them universally. How do we know that it enlightens them universally? Because it possesses them universally. How do we know that it possesses them universally? Because it accepts sacrifices from them universally. How do we know that it accepts sacrifices from them universally? Because within the four seas, among all the people who live on grain,[1] there are none who do not feed their sacrificial oxen and sheep, fatten their dogs and pigs, prepare clean offerings of millet and wine, and sacrifice to the Lord on High and the spirits. Since Heaven possesses all the cities and people, how could it fail to love them?

Moreover I say that he who kills one innocent person will invariably suffer one misfortune. Who is it that kills the innocent person? It is a man. And who is it that sends down the misfortune? It is Heaven. If Heaven did not love the people of the world, then why would it send down misfortune simply because one man kills another? Thus I know that Heaven loves the people of the world.

He who obeys the will of Heaven will regard righteousness as right. He who disobeys the will of Heaven will regard force as right. What does it mean to regard righteousness as right?

Mo Tzu said: If one is in a large state, he will not attack a small state. If one is a member of a large family, he will not bully a small family. The strong will not oppress the weak; the eminent will not lord it over the humble; the cunning will not deceive the stupid. This, then, will bring benefit to Heaven on high, to the spirits in the middle realm, and to man below. And because these three types of benefits are realized, the fairest names in the world will be given to such a man, and he will be called a sage king. But a man who regards force as right is different. His words and actions will be directly op-

[1] I.e., the Chinese, as opposed to the nomadic tribes surrounding China.

posed to these, as though he were galloping off in the opposite direction. If he is in a large state, he will attack a small state. If he is a member of a large family, he will bully small families. The strong will oppress the weak; the eminent will lord it over the humble; the cunning will deceive the stupid. This will bring no benefit to Heaven on high, to the spirits in the middle realm, or to man below. And because none of these three types of benefits are realized, the foulest names in the world will be given to such a man, and he will be called an evil king.

Mo Tzu said: The will of Heaven is to me like a compass to a wheelwright or a square to a carpenter. The wheelwright and the carpenter use their compass and square to measure what is round or square for the world, saying, "What fits these measurements is right; what does not fit them is wrong." Now the books of the gentlemen of the world are too numerous to be listed, and their sayings too many to be examined in full. Among the highest circles the gentlemen lecture to the feudal lords, and in lower circles they expound to men of honor. And yet on matters of benevolence and righteousness they are far apart. How do I know? Because I measure them by the clearest standard in the world [i.e., the will of Heaven.]

PART II

(SECTION 27)

Mo Tzu said: Now if the gentlemen of today wish to practice benevolence and righteousness, they must not fail to examine the origin of righteousness. If they must not fail to examine the origin of righteousness, then what is the origin of righteousness?

Mo Tzu said: Righteousness does not originate with the stupid and humble, but with the eminent and wise. How do we know that righteousness does not originate with the stupid and humble, but with the eminent and wise? Righteousness means doing what is right. How do we know that righteousness means doing what is right? Because when there is righteousness in the world, then the world is well ordered, but when there is no righteousness, then it is in disorder. Therefore we know that righteousness means doing what is right. Now the stupid and humble cannot decide what is right for the eminent and wise. There must first be the eminent and wise, who can then decide what is right for the stupid and humble. Therefore we know that righteousness does not originate with the stupid and humble, but with the eminent and wise.

Then who is eminent and who is wise? Heaven is pure eminence and pure wisdom. Therefore righteousness in fact originates with Heaven.

Now people in the world say: "It is perfectly obvious that the Son of Heaven is more eminent than the feudal lords and that the feudal lords are more eminent than the ministers. But we do not know that Heaven is more eminent and wise than the Son of Heaven!"

Mo Tzu said: I know that Heaven is more eminent and wise than the Son of Heaven for this reason: If the Son of Heaven does something good, Heaven has the power to reward him, and if he does something bad, Heaven has the power to punish him. If the Son of Heaven is suffering from some illness or misfortune, he must fast and purify himself, prepare clean offerings of wine and millet, and make sacrifices to Heaven and the spirits, and then Heaven will take away the affliction. But I have never heard of Heaven praying for blessings from the Son of Heaven. So I know that Heaven is more eminent and wise than the Son of Heaven. But this is not all. I also know it from one of the books of the former kings which explains the enlightened and unfathomable Way of Heaven in these words:

> Enlightened and wise is Heaven,
> Looking down upon and governing the world below.[2]

This, then, tells us that Heaven is more eminent and wise than the Son of Heaven. I do not know whether there is something even more eminent and wise than Heaven. But, as I have said, Heaven is pure eminence and wisdom. Therefore righteousness in fact originates with Heaven. So Mo Tzu said: If the gentlemen of the world truly desire to honor the Way, benefit the people, and search out the basis of benevolence and righteousness, then they must not fail to obey the will of Heaven.

If one must not fail to obey the will of Heaven, then what does Heaven desire and what does it hate?

Mo Tzu said: The will of Heaven does not desire that large states attack small ones, that large families overthrow small ones, that the strong oppress the weak, the cunning deceive the stupid, or the eminent lord it over the humble. This is what Heaven does *not* desire. But this is not all. It desires that among men those who have strength will work for others, those who understand the Way will teach others, and those who possess wealth will share it with others. It also desires that those above will diligently attend to matters of government, and those below will diligently carry out their tasks. If those

---

[2] Probably a reference to the opening lines of "Hsiao ming" (Mao text no. 207), *Hsiao ya* section, *Book of Odes*, though the text in the present version of the *Odes* is slightly different.

above diligently attend to matters of government, then the state will be well ordered. If those below diligently carry out their tasks, then there will be enough wealth and goods. If the state is well ordered and there are enough wealth and goods, then it will be possible to prepare clean offerings of wine and millet and to sacrifice to Heaven and the spirits within the state, and to provide circlets and other ornaments of jade and pearl by which to carry on diplomatic relations with surrounding states. When the state need not worry about the other feudal lords rising in anger against it or about armed clashes on its borders, when it can devote its efforts to feeding the hungry and giving rest to the weary at home and taking care of its own subjects, then its rulers and superiors will be generous and its subordinates and subjects loyal, its fathers and older brothers loving and its sons and younger brothers filial. Therefore, if one clearly understands how to obey the will of Heaven and put it into practice in the world at large, then the government will be well ordered, the population harmonious, the state rich, and wealth and goods plentiful. The people will all have warm clothes and plenty to eat, and will live in comfort and peace, free from care. Therefore Mo Tzu said: If the gentlemen of today truly desire to honor the Way, benefit the people, and search out the basis of benevolence and righteousness, then they must not fail to obey the will of Heaven.

Now the way in which Heaven holds possession of the world is no different from the way in which a ruler or a feudal lord holds possession of all within the four borders of his domain. When a ruler or a feudal lord holds possession of the land within the four borders of his domain, does he desire that his subjects should strive to harm each other? If he is a member of a large state and attacks a small state, if he is a member of a large family and overthrows a small family, though he may hope thereby to win reward and praise, he will never succeed, but will suffer punishment instead. Now the way in which Heaven holds possession of the world is no different. If one lives in a large state and leads it to attack a small one, if one lives in a large city and leads it to attack a small city, though one may hope thereby to win blessing and reward from Heaven, he will never succeed, but instead will call down upon himself misfortune and disaster. Thus, if men do not do what Heaven desires, but instead do what Heaven does not desire, then Heaven will likewise not do what men desire, but instead will do what men do not desire. What is it that men do not desire? Sickness, misfortune, and disaster. Thus, if one does not do what Heaven desires, but instead does what Heaven does not desire, this is simply to lead the multitudes of the world in pursuing the path to misfortune and disaster.

Therefore the sage kings of antiquity sought to understand clearly what Heaven and the spirits would bless, and to avoid what Heaven and the spirits hate, and in this way they worked to promote what is beneficial to the world and eliminate what is harmful. Thus Heaven sent forth its heat and cold in season, the four seasons proceeded in order, the yin and yang, rain and dew were timely, the five grains ripened, the six types of domestic animals[3] grew to maturity, and disease, pestilence, and famine did not occur. Therefore Mo Tzu said: If the gentlemen of today truly desire to honor the Way, benefit the people, and search out the basis of benevolence and righteousness, then they must not fail to obey the will of Heaven.

In the world there are those who are unbenevolent and ill-

---

[3] Horses, cattle, sheep, swine, fowl, and dogs. Dogs were raised to be eaten.

omened. If a son does not serve his father, a younger brother does not serve his older brother, or a subject does not serve his lord, then all the gentlemen of the world will call him ill-omened. Now Heaven loves the world universally and seeks to bring mutual benefit to all creatures. There is not so much as the tip of a hair which is not the work of Heaven. And since the people enjoy all these benefits, may we not say that its love for them is generous indeed? Yet in the case of Heaven alone they do nothing to repay this love, but even fail to perceive that they are unbenevolent and ill-omened. Therefore I say that gentlemen understand trifling matters but fail to understand important ones.

Moreover, I know for the following reason that Heaven loves the people generously: It sets forth one after another the sun and moon, the stars and constellations to lighten and lead them; it orders the four seasons, spring, fall, winter, and summer, to regulate their lives; it sends down snow and frost, rain and dew, to nourish the five grains, hemp, and silk, so that the people may enjoy the benefit of them. It lays out the mountains and rivers, the ravines and valley streams, and makes known all affairs so as to ascertain the good or evil of the people. It establishes kings and lords to reward the worthy and punish the wicked, to gather together metal and wood, birds and beasts, and to see to the cultivation of the five grains, hemp, and silk, so that the people may have enough food and clothing. From ancient times to the present this has always been so.

Suppose there is a man who delights in and loves his son, and does everything within his power to benefit him. If the son, when he grows up, does nothing to repay his father, then all the gentlemen of the world will call him unbenevolent and ill-fated. Now Heaven loves the world universally and seeks to bring mutual benefit to all creatures. There is not so much as the tip of a hair which is not the work of Heaven. And since the people enjoy all these benefits, may we not say that its love for them is generous indeed? Yet in the case of Heaven alone they do nothing to repay this love, but even fail to perceive that they are unbenevolent and ill-fated. Therefore I say that gentlemen understand trifling matters but fail to understand important ones.

Yet this is not the only reason that I know that Heaven loves the people generously. If someone kills an innocent person, then Heaven will send down misfortune upon him. Who is it that kills the innocent person? A man. And who is it that sends down the misfortune? Heaven. If Heaven did not love the people generously, then what reason would it have to send down misfortune upon the murderer of an innocent person? Thus I know that Heaven loves the people generously.

Yet there is another reason that I know that Heaven loves the people generously. There are those who, by loving and benefiting others and obeying the will of Heaven, have won Heaven's reward. And there are those who, hating and injuring others and disobeying the will of Heaven, have incurred Heaven's punishment. Who were those who, loving and benefiting others and obeying the will of Heaven, won Heaven's reward? Yao, Shun, Yü, T'ang, Wen, and Wu, the sage kings of the Three Dynasties of antiquity. What did Yao, Shun, Yü, T'ang, Wen, and Wu devote themselves to? They devoted themselves to universality and shunned partiality. Universality means that if one is in a large state he will not attack a small state, and if one is a member of a large family he will not overthrow a small family. The strong will not oppress the weak, the many will not bully the few, the cunning will not deceive the stupid, and the eminent will not lord it over the humble. Examining such a policy, we find that it brought benefit to Heaven above, to the spirits in the middle realm, and to man below. And because, of these three types of benefits, there were none that were not realized, it was called heavenly virtue. All the fairest names in the world were given to such a ruler, and people said, "This is benevolence; this is righteousness! This is what it means to love and benefit others, to obey the will of Heaven, and to win Heaven's reward!"

But this is not all. Such deeds were recorded on bamboo and silk, engraved on metal and stone, inscribed on bowls and basins, and handed down to posterity in generations after. Why was this done? It was done so that men would know how these rulers loved and benefited others, obeyed the will of Heaven, and won Heaven's reward. Thus the ode "Huang Yi" says:

> God said to King Wen:
> I am won by your bright virtue.
> Though renowned, you do not make a display;
> Though the leader of the land, you do not change.
> Without considering, without thinking,
> You obey the laws of God.[4]

God admired the way King Wen obeyed his laws, and therefore gave him possession of the realm of Yin as a reward, honoring him with the position of Son of Heaven and enriching him with the world, and even today the sound of his praise never ceases. So we know who those were who, loving and benefiting others and obeying the will of Heaven, won Heaven's reward.

Who were those who, hating and injuring others and dis-

[4] Book of Odes, *Ta ya* section, "Huang Yi" (Mao text no. 241).

obeying the will of Heaven, incurred Heaven's punishment? Chieh, Chou, Yu, and Li, the evil kings of the Three Dynasties of antiquity. What did Chieh, Chou, Yu, and Li devote themselves to? They devoted themselves to partiality and spurned universality. Partiality means that if one is in a large state he will attack a small state, and if one is a member of a large family, he will overthrow small families. The strong will oppress the weak, the many will bully the few, the cunning will deceive the stupid, and the eminent will lord it over the humble. Examining such a policy, we find that it brought no benefit to Heaven above, to the spirits in the middle realm, or to man below. And because it failed to realize these three types of benefits, it was called an offense against Heaven. All the foulest names in the world were given to such a ruler, and people said, "This is not benevolence; this is not righteousness! This is what it means to hate and injure others, to disobey the will of Heaven, and to incur Heaven's punishment!"

But this is not all. Such deeds were recorded on bamboo and silk, engraved on metal and stone, inscribed on bowls and basins, and handed down to posterity in generations after. Why was this done? It was done so that men would know how these rulers hated and injured others, disobeyed the will of Heaven, and incurred Heaven's punishment. Thus the "Great Declaration" [5] says: "Chou sits with his legs sprawled out and refuses to serve the Lord on High. He neglects the spirits of the former kings and fails to sacrifice to them. And yet he insists, 'I have the mandate of Heaven!' He gives himself up to insult and tyranny, and Heaven therefore casts him away and will not protect him." If we examine the matter, we will realize that Heaven cast Chou away and would not protect

---

[5] A lost section of the *Book of Documents*. The section by this name in the present text of the *Documents* is spurious.

him because he disobeyed the will of Heaven. So we know who those were who, hating and injuring others and disobeying the will of Heaven, incurred Heaven's punishment.

Therefore Mo Tzu said: The will of Heaven is to me like a compass to a wheelwright or a square to a carpenter. The wheelwright uses his compass to test the roundness of every object in the world, saying, "What matches the line of my compass I say is round. What does not match my compass I say is not round." Therefore he can tell in every case whether a thing is round or not, because he has a standard for roundness. The carpenter uses his square to test the squareness of every object in the world, saying, "What matches my square is square. What does not match my square is not square." Therefore he can tell in every case whether a thing is square or not, because he has a standard for squareness.

In the same way Mo Tzu uses the will of Heaven to measure the government of the rulers and ministers above, and the writings and words of the multitudes below. He observes their actions, and if they obey the will of Heaven, he calls them good actions, but if they disobey the will of Heaven, he calls them bad actions. He observes their words, and if they obey the will of Heaven, he calls them good words, but if they disobey the will of Heaven, he calls them bad words. He observes their government, and if it obeys the will of Heaven, he calls it good government, but if it disobeys the will of Heaven, he calls it bad government. Thus he employs this as a standard, establishes it as a measurement, and with it measures the benevolence or unbenevolence of the rulers and ministers of the world, and it is as easy as telling black from white. Therefore Mo Tzu said: If the rulers, ministers, and gentlemen of the world truly desire to honor the Way, benefit

the people, and search out the basis of benevolence and righteousness, then they must not fail to obey the will of Heaven,
for obedience to the will of Heaven is the standard of righteousness.

Mo Tzu said: Now that the sage kings of the Three Dynasties of antiquity have passed away and the world has forgotten their principles, the feudal lords regard might as right. So we have rulers and superiors who are not generous and subordinates and subjects who are not loyal, fathers and sons, younger and older brothers who are not loving or filial, brotherly or respectful, virtuous or good. The leaders of the state do not diligently attend to affairs of government, and the humble people do not diligently pursue their tasks. The people give themselves up to evil, violence, thievery, and rebellion, using weapons, knives, poison, fire, and water to assault innocent persons on the roads and byways and seize their carriages and horses, robes and furs, for their own benefit. All of these conditions come about for the same reason, and as a result the world is in disorder.

Now why do we have this state of affairs? It all comes about because people are in doubt as to whether ghosts and spirits exist or not, and do not realize that ghosts and spirits have the power to reward the worthy and punish the wicked. If we could only make all the people in the world believe that the ghosts and spirits have the power to reward the worthy and punish the wicked, then how could there be any disorder in the world?

Those who claim that ghosts do not exist say: "Of course

there is no such thing!", and morning and evening they preach this doctrine to the world, spreading skepticism among the people and causing them to be in doubt as to whether ghosts and spirits exist or not. Thus the world becomes disordered. Therefore Mo Tzu said: If the rulers, ministers, and gentlemen of the world today truly desire to promote what is beneficial to the world and eliminate what is harmful, they must face this question of whether ghosts and spirits exist or not and examine it.

It is clear that one must examine this question of whether ghosts and spirits exist or not. Well then, if the examination is to be sound, what method should we use?

Mo Tzu said: The way to determine whether something exists or not is to find out whether people actually know from the evidence of their own ears and eyes whether it exists, and use this as a standard. If someone has actually heard it and seen it, then we must assume that it exists. But if no one has heard or seen it, then we must assume that it does not exist. If this is to be our method, then why don't we try going to some village or community and asking? If from antiquity to today, from the beginning of mankind to the present, there have been people who have seen ghostlike and spiritlike beings and heard their voices, then how can we say they don't exist? But if no one has seen or heard them, then how can we say they exist?

Now those who claim that ghosts do not exist say: "There are countless people in the world who say they have seen or heard ghostlike or spiritlike beings. But who among them has ever really seen or heard such a being?" [1]

Mo Tzu said: If we are to go by what many people have jointly seen and what many people have jointly heard, then

[1] The meaning of this sentence is doubtful.

there is the case of Tu Po. King Hsüan [traditional dates 827–783 B.C.] of the Chou dynasty put to death his minister Tu Po, though he had committed no crime. Tu Po said, "My lord, you are going to put me to death, though I have committed no crime. If the dead have no consciousness, that will be the end of the matter. But if the dead have consciousness, then before three years are over I will make you know it!" Three years later King Hsüan called together the feudal lords and went hunting at P'u. His party of several hundred hunting chariots and several thousand attendants filled the field. At midday Tu Po appeared, wearing a vermilion hat and robe, holding a vermilion bow and vermilion arrows, and riding in a plain chariot drawn by a white horse. He pursued King Hsüan and shot him in his chariot. The arrow pierced the king's heart and broke his back. He fell down in his chariot, slumped over his quiver, and died. At that time there were none among the Chou attendants who did not see what happened, and no one in distant regions who did not hear about it.[2] It was recorded in the spring and autumn annals of Chou,[3] rulers used it to instruct their subjects, and fathers to warn their sons, saying, "Be careful! Be circumspect! All those who kill innocent men will suffer misfortune and incur the punishment of the ghosts and spirits with just such rapidity!" If we examine what is written in the book, how can we doubt that ghosts and spirits exist?

And yet it is not only what is written in this book that proves it. Once long ago Duke Mu of Ch'in [659–620 B.C.][4]

[2] Mo Tzu uses the verb "to hear" at this point in the sense of "to hear the report of," which is hardly the same thing as hearing a voice or sound that would prove the existence of spirits.

[3] "Spring and autumn" is here a generic term for the season-by-season chronicles kept by the historiographers of the various states.

[4] The text says "Duke Mu of Cheng," but the legend is traditionally associated with Duke Mu of Ch'in.

was in his ancestral temple during the day, when a spirit entered the gate and turned to the left. It had the face of a man and the body of a bird, wore a white robe with black borders, and was very dignified and grave in appearance. When Duke Mu saw it, he was frightened and started to run away, but the spirit said, "Do not be afraid. God recognizes your enlightened virtue and has sent me to bestow upon you nineteen more years of life. He will make your state prosperous and your descendants numerous, and they shall not lose possession of Ch'in!" Duke Mu bowed twice, lowered his head, and said, "May I ask the name of this spirit?" and the spirit replied, "I am Kou Mang." If we are to accept as reliable what Duke Mu of Ch'in saw in person, then how can we doubt that ghosts and spirits exist?

And yet it is not only what is written in this book that proves it. In ancient times Duke Chien of Yen [504–492 B.C.] put to death his minister Chuang Tzu-i, though he had committed no crime. Chuang Tzu-i said, "My lord, you are going to put me to death, though I have committed no crime. If the dead have no consciousness, that will be the end of the matter. But if the dead have consciousness, then before three years are over I will make you know it!" A year later the ruler of Yen was about to set off in his chariot for Tsu. (Tsu in Yen is like She-chi in Ch'i, Sang-lin in Sung, and Yün-meng in Ch'u, a place where men and women gather to sightsee.)[5] At noon, just as the duke of Yen was about to set off on the road for Tsu, Chuang Tzu-i appeared carrying a vermilion staff and struck down the duke in his chariot. At that time there were none among the Yen attendants who did not see what hap-

---

[5] The sentence in parentheses is in the nature of a note, perhaps added by a later writer. The places mentioned were apparently the scenes of religious observances.

pened, and no one in distant regions who did not hear about it. It was recorded in the spring and autumn annals of Yen, and the feudal lords handed down the story, saying, "All those who kill innocent men will suffer misfortune and incur the punishment of the ghosts and spirits with just such rapidity!" If we examine what is written in the book, how can we doubt that ghosts and spirits exist?

And yet it is not only what is written in this book that proves it. Long ago, in the time of Pao, Lord Wen of Sung [610–589 B.C.], there was a minister named Kuan-ku the Invocator, who served in the ancestral temple of the state. Once a shaman appeared from the temple, bearing a club, and said, "Kuan-ku, what does this mean? The sacramental jades and circlets do not fulfill the proper standard, the offerings of wine and millet are impure, the sacrificial animals are not fat and flawless as they should be, and the ceremonies appropriate to the four seasons are not performed at the right times! Is this your doing or Pao's?" Kuan-ku replied, "Pao is an infant, still in swaddling clothes. What does he know of such matters? I am in charge, and it is all my doing!" Then the shaman raised his club and struck Kuan-ku, and he fell dead on the altar. At that time there were none of the Sung attendants who did not see what happened, and no one in distant regions who did not hear about it. It was recorded in the spring and autumn annals of Sung, and the feudal lords handed down the story, saying, "All who fail to conduct sacrifices with the proper respect and circumspection will incur the punishment of the ghosts and spirits with just such rapidity!" If we examine what is written in the book, how can we doubt that ghosts and spirits exist?

And yet it is not only what is written in this book that proves it. Long ago, in the time of Lord Chuang of Ch'i [794–731 B.C.], there were two ministers named Wang-li Kuo and

Chung-li Chiao. These two men had been engaged in a law-suit for three years, but no judgment had been handed down. Lord Chuang thought of executing them both, but he was afraid of killing an innocent man. He also thought of acquitting them both, but he was afraid of setting free one who was guilty. He therefore ordered the two men to bring a lamb and take an oath on the Ch'i altar of the soil. The two men agreed to take the oath of blood. The throat of the lamb was cut, its blood sprinkled on the altar, and Wang-li Kuo's version of the case read through to the end. Next Chung-li Chiao's version was read, but before it had been read half through, the lamb rose up, butted Chung-li Chiao, broke his leg,[6] and then struck him down on the altar. At that time there were none of the attendants of Ch'i who did not see what happened, and no one in distant regions who did not hear about it. It was recorded in the spring and autumn annals of Ch'i, and the feudal lords handed down the story, saying, "All those who take oaths in insincerity will incur the punishment of the ghosts and spirits with just such rapidity!" If we examine what is written in the book, how can we doubt that ghosts and spirits exist?

Therefore Mo Tzu said: Even in the deep valleys, the broad forests, the dark and distant places where no one lives, you must not fail to act with sincerity, for the ghosts and spirits will see you even there!

Now those who claim that ghosts do not exist say, "How can one rely upon the eyes and ears of the multitude in settling doubts? Can one hope to be a superior gentleman of the world and still trust the eyes and ears of the multitude?"

Mo Tzu said: If one is not to trust the eyes and ears of the multitude in settling doubts, then, may I ask, are the sage

---

[6] The text is somewhat garbled at this point.

kings of the Three Dynasties of antiquity, Yao, Shun, Yü, T'ang, Wen, and Wu, worthy to be accepted as a standard in such matters? Surely every man who is above the average will answer that they are. Therefore let us review for a moment the deeds of these sage kings.

In ancient times, after King Wu had attacked the state of Yin and punished its ruler, Chou, he ordered the feudal lords to divide up the sacrificial duties, saying, "Those who are closely related to the throne may participate in the inner worship; those distantly related may participate in the outer worship." It is clear that King Wu must have believed in the existence of ghosts and spirits, since, after attacking Yin and overthrowing Chou, he ordered the feudal lords to divide up the sacrificial duties in this way. If no ghosts or spirits existed, then why would King Wu have had the sacrificial duties divided up?

And yet it is not only the deeds of King Wu that prove their existence. The sage kings of old always bestowed rewards at the ancestral temple and meted out punishment at the altar of the soil. Why were rewards bestowed at the ancestral temple? To announce to the spirits that the division of rewards was fair. Why were punishments meted out at the altar of the soil? To announce to the spirits that the sentence was just.

And yet it is not only what is written in the books about King Wu that proves their existence. In ancient times, on the day when the rulers of Yü, Hsia, Shang, and Chou, the sage kings of the Three Dynasties, first established their states and set up their capitals, they always selected a site for the main altar of the state, and constructed an ancestral temple there. They would select a site where the trees were particularly fine and luxuriant, and there in the grove set up the altar of the soil. Then they would select the most kind, filial, virtuous, and good men among the elders of the state to act as invocators of the temple; select the plumpest, most perfectly shaped and colored among the six domestic animals to be sacrificial victims; provide jade circlets, badges, and pendants of the proper quality and number; and select the most fragrant and yellow of the five grains to be used for the offerings of wine and millet, the quality of the wine and millet varying with the abundance of the year. This was how the sage kings of ancient times, when they ruled the world, put the affairs of the ghosts and spirits first, and those of the people last. Therefore it was said that, when the government offices provide the implements of state, they must first see to it that the proper vessels and robes for use in the sacrifices are fully stocked in the storehouses, that the invocators of the temple and other officials in charge of sacrifices have been appointed in full number in the court, and that the animals to be used as sacrificial victims have been separated from the common herds. Since the ancient sage kings conducted their government in this fashion, they must have believed in the existence of ghosts and spirits.

Such was their deep concern for the service of the ghosts and spirits. But, fearing that their sons and grandsons in later ages would not understand this, they made a record of it on bamboo and silk to be handed down to posterity. Again, fearing that these might rot and become lost, so that later ages would have no way to learn what had been written on them, they inscribed it on bowls and basins, and engraved it on metal and stone as well. Still they feared that their descendants might not show the proper reverence, and therefore fail to obtain blessing. Therefore, in the books of the former kings, among the words of the sages, we find, within one scroll of silk or one bundle of bamboo writing slips, repeated mentions of the existence of ghosts and spirits. Why is this? Because this is what the sage kings were most concerned about. Now those who claim that ghosts do not exist and go about saying that there are no such things as ghosts or spirits are turning their backs on the concerns of the sage kings. This is surely not the way of a true gentleman!

Those who claim that ghosts do not exist say, "These books of the former kings, these words of the sages, which within one scroll of silk or one bundle of bamboo writing slips repeatedly mention the existence of ghosts and spirits—tell us, what books are they?"

Mo Tzu said: Among the books of Chou there are the "Greater Odes," for instance. The "Greater Odes" says:

> King Wen is on high,
> He shines in Heaven!
> Chou is an old people
> But its charge is new.
> The leaders of Chou became illustrious.
> Was not God's charge timely given?
> King Wen ascends and descends
> On the left and right of God.
> Majestic is King Wen,
> His good fame never ceases.[7]

If ghosts and spirits do not exist, then how could King Wen, who was already dead, be "on the left and right of God?" So I know that the books of Chou recognize the existence of ghosts.

But if there are ghosts in the books of Chou, but none in the books of Shang, then we do not have sufficient proof for our argument. Therefore let us try going back a little further and

[7] *Book of Odes,* "Greater Odes" or *Ta ya* section, "Wen wang" (Mao text no. 235).

examining the books of Shang. There we find it written: "Ah, in ancient times, before the rulers of Hsia were visited by misfortune, among all the beasts and living creatures, even to the birds that fly, there were none that did not follow the proper way. How much more those creatures with the faces of men! Would they have dared to have contrary hearts? Likewise the ghosts and spirits of the mountains and rivers—would any of them have dared to be restless? So the rulers of Hsia, with reverence and sincerity, brought harmony to the world and guarded the land below." [8] Now if we examine the reasons that the ghosts and spirits did not dare to be restless, we find that it is because they were aiding Yü in his rule. So I knew that the books of Shang recognize the existence of ghosts.

But if there are ghosts in the books of Shang, but none in the books of Hsia, then we do not have sufficient proof for our argument. Therefore let us try going back a little further and examining the books of Hsia. The "Declaration of Yü" says: "There was a great battle at Kan. The king summoned the six commanders of the left and right and made this declaration to the army, saying: 'The lord of Hu violates the five elements and discards the three standards [of Heaven, earth, and man]. Heaven therefore cuts off his mandate!' He also said: 'This day I shall fight with the lord of Hu for the day's fate. You ministers, officers, and commoners, it is not that I covet your fields or guarded lands. I am only respectfully carrying out Heaven's punishment. If you on the left do not do your duty on the left, or if you on the right do not do your duty on the right, you will not be carrying out my orders. If you charioteers do not correctly manage your horses, you will

---

[8] Mo Tzu is apparently quoting from some lost section of the *Book of Documents*. It is possible that the quotation should end with the word "restless," and that the sentence which follows is Mo Tzu's comment.

not be carrying out my orders. Rewards will be conferred in the ancestral temple and punishments meted out at the altar of the soil.' " [9] Why were rewards conferred at the ancestral temple? To show that the division of rewards was fair. Why were punishments meted out at the altar of the soil? To show that the sentences were just. Because the ancient sage kings believed that it was through the ghosts and spirits that the worthy were rewarded and the evil punished, they invariably conferred rewards in the ancestral temple and meted out punishments at the altar of the soil. So I know that the books of Hsia recognize the existence of ghosts.

Thus, first in the books of Hsia and then in the books of Shang and Chou, we find the existence of ghosts and spirits mentioned again and again. Why is this? Because the sage kings were deeply concerned about such matters. If we examine what is written in these books, how can we doubt that ghosts and spirits exist?

It is said that in ancient times, on the propitious day *ting-mao*, the Chou people offered prayers to the altar of the soil and the four quarters, and yearly prayers to the ancestors, in order to prolong the years of their life. If there were no ghosts or spirits, then how could they hope in this way to prolong their lives? [10]

Therefore Mo Tzu said: If the fact that the ghosts and spirits reward the worthy and punish the evil can be made a cornerstone of policy in the state and impressed upon the

[9] The passage, with some textual variations, comprises almost all of the section known as the "Declaration at Kan" in the present *Book of Documents*.

[10] The text of this passage and its relation to what comes before and after are very doubtful. *Ting-mao* is the designation of one of the days in the sixty-day cycle in use for recording dates at least from Shang times on.

common people, it will provide a means to bring order to the state and benefit to the people. When there is corruption among the officials and heads of bureaus, or illicit relations between men and women, the ghosts and spirits will see it. When the people give themselves up to evil and violence, thievery and rebellion, using weapons, knives, poison, fire, and water to assault innocent persons on the roads and byways and seize their carriages, horses, robes, and furs for their own benefit, the ghosts and spirits will see this too. Therefore the officials and heads of bureaus will not dare to be corrupt. When they see good, they will not dare to withhold reward, and when they see evil, they will not dare to withhold punishment. And the people who give themselves up to evil and violence, thievery and rebellion, using weapons, knives, poison, fire, and water to assault innocent persons on the roads and byways and seize their carriages, horses, robes, and furs for their own benefit—all these people will as a result cease their activities,[11] and the world will be well ordered.

Beneath the sharp eyes of the ghosts and spirits, dark caves and broad swamps, mountain forests and deep valleys are no protection. The ghosts and spirits will invariably spy you out and know what you have done. Before the punishment of the ghosts and spirits, wealth, honor, strength of numbers, bravery, might, strong armor, and sharp weapons are of no avail, for the punishment of the ghosts and spirits will overcome all these.

Do you think it is not so? In ancient times King Chieh of the Hsia dynasty was honored with the position of Son of Heaven, and possessed all the wealth of the world. Yet above

---

[11] Twenty-one characters, representing some sort of textual garble, have been omitted at this point.

he blasphemed against Heaven and despised the spirits, while below he abused and slaughtered the common people.[12] Thereupon Heaven commanded T'ang to carry out its enlightened punishment. T'ang, with his nine chariots arranged in the Bird Formation and the Wild Goose March, ascended Ta-tsan, scattered the forces of Hsia, entered the suburbs of the capital, and with his own hands captured T'ui-i Ta-hsi. Thus in ancient times King Chieh of the Hsia was honored with the position of Son of Heaven, and possessed all the wealth of the world; he had in his service a man of daring and strength named T'ui-i Ta-hsi who could tear apart a live rhinoceros or tiger and directed the killing of others; and he had such millions of soldiers that they filled the lowlands and hills. And yet he could not ward off the punishment of the ghosts and spirits. So I know from this that before the punishment of the ghosts and spirits, wealth, honor, strength of numbers, bravery, might, strong armor, and sharp weapons are of no avail.

Yet this is not all. In ancient times King Chou of the Yin dynasty was honored with the position of Son of Heaven, and possessed all the wealth of the world. Yet above he blasphemed against Heaven and despised the spirits, while below he abused and slaughtered the common people. He cast aside the aged, murdered little children, roasted innocent men alive, and cut open pregnant women. The common people and the aged, the widows and widowers wept and cried, but they had no one to appeal to. Thereupon Heaven commanded King Wu to carry out its enlightened punishment. King Wu, with a hundred select chariots and four hundred brave warriors, announced his intentions to the other lords and, with the seals of authority, reviewed the troops. He fought with the men of Yin

---

[12] A garble of eight characters has been omitted. The text of this whole paragraph is in very poor condition.

in the field of Mu, and with his own hands captured Fei Chung and E Lai, and the multitude deserted and ran away. King Wu rushed after them into the palace,[13] and cut off Chou's head and hung it from a red ring mounted on a white banner, thus carrying out punishment for the feudal lords of the world. So in ancient times King Chou was honored with the position of Son of Heaven, and possessed all the wealth of the world; he had in his service men of daring and strength such as Fei Chung, E Lai, and Hu, the marquis of Ch'ung, who directed the killing of others; and he had such millions of soldiers that they filled the lowlands and hills. And yet he could not ward off the punishment of the ghosts and spirits. So I know from this that before the punishment of the ghosts and spirits, wealth, honor, strength of numbers, bravery, might, strong armor, and sharp weapons are of no avail.

Moreover the words of Ch'in Ai tell us: "Attaining virtue is not a small matter; wiping out a family is not a large one." [14] That is to say, when the ghosts and spirits confer rewards, no matter is too small to be rewarded. And when the ghosts and spirits mete out punishment, no consideration is great enough to interfere.

Those who claim that ghosts do not exist say, "This not only fails to benefit parents, but actually does harm to filial sons, does it not?" [15]

Mo Tzu said: The ghosts and spirits of past and present are of three kinds only: the spirits of Heaven, the spirits of the mountains and rivers, and the ghosts of men who have died. Now it sometimes happens, it is true, that a son dies

---

[13] A four-character garble has been omitted at this point.

[14] Perhaps from a lost section of the *Book of Documents*.

[15] I do not fully understand the objection of the anti-ghost party at this point, nor what connection it has with what comes before and after. The statement apparently concerns family sacrifices to deceased parents.

before his father, or a younger brother before his older brother. And yet, as the old saying of the world has it, "He who is born first dies first." So those who die first will be either one's father or one's mother, one's elder brother or one's elder sister. Now when we prepare pure wine and millet and offer them with reverence and circumspection, if ghosts and spirits really exist, then we are thereby providing food and drink for our fathers, mothers, elder brothers, and elder sisters. Is this not a great benefit?

Of course if ghosts and spirits do not really exist, then it would seem that we are wasting the materials we use, the wine and millet. But though we expend them, it is not as though we were simply pouring the wine in a sewage ditch and throwing the millet away. For the members of the family and the people of the community can all gather to drink and eat them. Therefore, though no ghosts or spirits existed at all, we would still have the opportunity to gather together a pleasant group and make friends with the people of the community.

Those who claim that ghosts do not exist say, "There has never been any such thing as ghosts and spirits. Therefore I shall not expend my wealth on wine, millet, and sacrificial animals. It is not that I begrudge the expense of such things, but what is to be accomplished by offering them?" This is to oppose what is written in the books of the sage kings and violate the way of a filial son of the people. Such people claim to be the superior men of the world, but this is surely not the way to be a superior man!

Therefore Mo Tzu said: Now when I perform sacrifices, it is not as though I were pouring the wine in a sewage ditch and throwing the millet away. Above I am seeking the blessing of the ghosts and spirits, while below I am gathering together a pleasant group and making friends with the people of the community. And if the ghosts and spirits really exist, then I am able to provide food and drink for my father, my mother, and my elder brothers and sisters. Is this not beneficial to the whole world?[16]

Therefore Mo Tzu said: If the rulers, ministers, and gentlemen of the world truly desire to promote what is beneficial to the world and eliminate what is harmful, they must believe in the existence of ghosts and spirits and honor them accordingly, for this is the way of the sage kings.

[16] In this closing section Mo Tzu speaks as though he were not himself wholly convinced of the existence of ghosts and spirits.

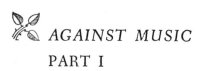

AGAINST MUSIC
PART I
(SECTION 32)

It is the business of the benevolent man to seek to promote what is beneficial to the world, to eliminate what is harmful, and to provide a model for the world. What benefits men he will carry out; what does not benefit men he will leave alone. Moreover, when the benevolent man plans for the benefit of the world, he does not consider merely what will please the eye, delight the ear, gratify the mouth, and give ease to the body. If in order to gratify the senses he has to deprive the people of the wealth needed for their food and clothing, then the benevolent man will not do so. Therefore Mo Tzu condemns music[1] not because the sound of the great bells and rolling drums, the zithers and pipes, is not delightful; not because the sight of the carvings and ornaments is not beautiful; not because the taste of the fried and broiled meats is not delicious; and not because lofty towers, broad pavilions, and secluded halls are not comfortable to live in. But though the body finds comfort, the mouth gratification, the eye pleasure, and the ear delight, yet if we examine the matter, we will find that such things are not in accordance with the ways of the sage kings, and if we consider the welfare of the world we

[1] The term "music" in ancient China customarily denoted not only music itself, but dances and pantomimes that accompanied it. Here, however, Mo Tzu seems to be using the term even more broadly to include the lavish banquets and sumptuous surroundings that in his mind were associated with the musical entertainments of the aristocracy.

will find that they bring no benefit to the common people. Therefore Mo Tzu said: Making music is wrong!

Now if the rulers and ministers want musical instruments to use in their government activities, they cannot extract them from the sea water, like salt, or dig them out of the ground, like ore. Inevitably, therefore, they must lay heavy taxes upon the common people before they can enjoy the sound of great bells, rolling drums, zithers, and pipes. In ancient times the sage kings likewise laid heavy taxes on the people, but this was for the purpose of making boats and carts, and when they were completed and people asked, "What are these for?" the sage kings replied, "The boats are for use on water, and the carts for use on land, so that gentlemen may rest their feet and laborers spare their shoulders." So the common people paid their taxes and levies and did not dare to grumble. Why? Because they knew that the taxes would be used for the benefit of the people. Now if musical instruments were also used for the benefit of the people, I would not venture to condemn them. Indeed, if they were as useful as the boats and carts of the sage kings, I would certainly not venture to condemn them.

There are three things the people worry about: that when they are hungry they will have no food, when they are cold they will have no clothing, and when they are weary they will have no rest. These are the three great worries of the people. Now let us try sounding the great bells, striking the rolling drums, strumming the zithers, blowing the pipes, and waving the shields and axes in the war dance. Does this do anything to provide food and clothing for the people? I hardly think so. But let us leave that point for the moment.

Now there are great states that attack small ones, and great families that molest small ones. The strong oppress the weak, the many tyrannize the few, the cunning deceive the stupid, the eminent lord it over the humble, and bandits and thieves rise up on all sides and cannot be suppressed. Now let us try sounding the great bells, striking the rolling drums, strumming the zithers, blowing the pipes, and waving the shields and axes in the war dance. Does this do anything to rescue the world from chaos and restore it to order? I hardly think so. Therefore Mo Tzu said: If you try to promote what is beneficial to the world and eliminate what is harmful by laying heavy taxes on the people for the purpose of making bells, drums, zithers, and pipes, you will get nowhere. So Mo Tzu said: Making music is wrong!

Now the rulers and ministers, seated in their lofty towers and broad pavilions, look about them, and there are the bells, hanging like huge cauldrons. But unless the bells are struck, how can the rulers get any delight out of them? Therefore it is obvious that the rulers must have someone to strike the bells. But they cannot employ old men or young boys, since their eyes and ears are not keen enough and their arms are not strong, and they cannot make the sounds harmonious or see to strike the bells front and back. Therefore the rulers must have young people in their prime, whose eyes and ears are keen and whose arms are so strong that they can make the sounds harmonious and see to strike the bells front and back. If they employ young men, then they will be taking them away from their plowing and planting, and if they employ young women, they will be taking them away from their weaving and spinning. Yet the rulers and ministers will have their music, though their music-making interferes to such an extent with the people's efforts to produce food and clothing! Therefore Mo Tzu said: Making music is wrong!

Now let us suppose that the great bells, rolling drums, zithers, and pipes have all been provided. Still if the rulers and ministers sit quietly all alone and listen to the performance, how can they get any delight out of it? Therefore it is obvious that they must listen in the company of others, either humble men or gentlemen. If they listen in the company of gentlemen, then they will be keeping the gentlemen from attending to affairs of state, while if they listen in the company of humble men, they will be keeping the humble men from pursuing their tasks. Yet the rulers and ministers will have their music, though their music-making interferes to such an extent with the people's efforts to produce food and clothing! Therefore Mo Tzu said: Making music is wrong!

In former times Duke K'ang of Ch'i [404–379 B.C.] loved the music of the Wan dance.[2] The Wan dancers cannot wear robes of cheap cloth or eat coarse food, for it is said that unless they have the finest food and drink, their faces and complexions will not be fit to look at, and unless they have beautiful clothing, their figures and movements will not be worth watching. Therefore the Wan dancers ate only millet and meat, and wore only robes of patterned and embroidered silk. They did nothing to help produce food or clothing, but lived entirely off the efforts of others. Yet the rulers and ministers will have their music, though their music-making interferes to such an extent with the people's efforts to produce food and clothing! Therefore Mo Tzu said: Making music is wrong!

Now man is basically different from the beasts, birds, and insects. The beasts, birds, and insects have feathers and fur for their robes and coats, hoofs and claws for their leggings and shoes, and grass and water for their food and drink. Therefore the male need not plow or plant, the female need

[2] For a summary of the little that is known about this ancient type of dance, see Arthur Waley, *Book of Songs* (London, Allen and Unwin, 1937; reprint, New York, Grove Press, 1960), pp. 338–40.

not weave or spin, and still they have plenty of food and clothing. But man is different from such creatures. If a man exerts his strength, he may live, but if he does not, he cannot live. If the gentlemen do not diligently attend to affairs of state, the government will fall into disorder, and if humble men do not diligently pursue their tasks, there will not be enough wealth and goods.

If the gentlemen of the world do not believe what I say, then let us try enumerating the various duties of the people of the world and see how music interferes with them. The rulers and ministers must appear at court early and retire late, hearing lawsuits and attending to affairs of government—this is their duty. The gentlemen must exhaust the strength of their limbs and employ to the fullest the wisdom of their minds, directing bureaus within the government and abroad, collecting taxes on the barriers and markets and on the resources of the hills, forests, lakes, and fish weirs, so that the granaries and treasuries will be full—this is their duty. The farmers must leave home early and return late, sowing seed, planting trees, and gathering large crops of vegetables and grain—this is their duty. Women must rise early and go to bed late, spinning, weaving, producing large quantities of hemp, silk, and other fibers, and preparing cloth—this is their duty. Now if those who occupy the position of rulers and ministers are fond of music and spend their time listening to it, then they will not be able to appear at court early and retire late, or hear lawsuits and attend to affairs of government, and as a result the state will fall into disorder and its altars of the soil and grain will be in danger. If those who occupy the position of gentlemen are fond of music and spend their time listening to it, then they will be unable to exhaust the strength of their limbs and employ to the fullest the wisdom of their minds in directing bureaus within the government and abroad, collecting taxes on the barriers and markets and on the resources of the hills, forests, lakes, and fish weirs, in order to fill the granaries and treasuries, and as a result the granaries and treasuries will not be filled. If those who occupy the position of farmers are fond of music and spend their time listening to it,[3] then they will be unable to leave home early and return late, sowing seed, planting trees, and gathering large crops of vegetables and grain, and as a result there will be a lack of vegetables and grain. If women are fond of music and spend their time listening to it, then they will be unable to rise early and go to bed late, spinning, weaving, producing large quantities of hemp, silk, and other fibers, and preparing cloth, and as a result there will not be enough cloth. If you ask what it is that has caused the ruler to neglect the affairs of government and the humble man to neglect his tasks, the answer is music. Therefore Mo Tzu said: Making music is wrong!

How do we know that this is so? The proof is found among the books of the former kings, in T'ang's "Code of Punishment," where it says: "Constant dancing in the palace—this is the way of shamans! As a punishment, gentlemen shall be fined two measures of silk, but for common men the fine shall be two hundred pieces of yellow silk."[4] It also says: "Alas, all this dancing! The sound of the pipes is loud and clear. The Lord on High does not aid him, and the nine

---

[3] The possibility of farmers and peasant women in ancient China becoming fatally infatuated with the music of the aristocracy seems so remote that we must suppose that Mo Tzu's argument from here on is merely rhetorical.

[4] Apparently from a lost section of the *Book of Documents*. The meaning of the last sentence is very doubtful.

districts are lost to him.[5] The Lord on High does not approve him, but sends down a hundred misfortunes. His house will be destroyed." If we examine the reason why he lost the nine districts, we will find that it was because he idly spent his time arranging elaborate musical performances.

The "Wu kuan" says: "Ch'i[6] gave himself up to pleasure and music, eating and drinking in the fields. *Ch'iang-ch-iang*, the flutes and chimes sounded in unison! He drowned himself in wine and behaved indecently by eating in the fields. Splendid was the Wan dance, but Heaven clearly heard the sound and Heaven did not approve." So it was not approved by Heaven and the spirits above, and brought no benefit to the people below.

Therefore Mo Tzu said: If the rulers, ministers, and gentlemen of the world truly desire to promote what is beneficial to the world and eliminate what is harmful, they must prohibit and put a stop to this thing called music!

[5] The nine districts that were supposed to have made up the China of ancient times. The "he" of the quotation is presumably Chieh, the evil ruler of the Hsia who was overthrown by T'ang.

[6] The identity of this man and the source of the quotation are a matter of controversy. The text of all three quotations is in very poor condition.

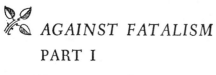

AGAINST FATALISM

PART I

(SECTION 35)

Mo Tzu said: These days the rulers and high officials who govern the nation all desire their states to be rich, their population to be numerous, and their administration to be well ordered. And yet what they achieve is not wealth but poverty, not a numerous population but a meager one, not order but chaos. In actual fact, they fail to get what they seek and achieve what they abhor. Why is this? Mo Tzu said: It is because of the large number of fatalists among the people.

The advocates of fatalism say, "If fate decrees that the state will be wealthy, it will be wealthy; if it decrees that it will be poor, it will be poor. If it decrees that the population will be numerous, it will be numerous; if it decrees that it will be meager, it will be meager. If it decrees that there will be order, there will be order; if it decrees that there will be chaos, there will be chaos. If it decrees that a man will have a long life, he will have a long life; if it decrees that he will die young, he will die young. Though a man tries to combat fate, what can he do?" They expound such doctrines to the rulers and high officials, and keep the people from pursuing their tasks. Hence the fatalists are lacking in benevolence, and their words must therefore be carefully examined.

Now how are we to go about examining their doctrines? Mo Tzu said: We must set up a standard of judgment, for to try to speak without a standard of judgment is like trying to establish the direction of sunrise and sunset with a revolving potter's wheel. It will be impossible to determine the difference between what is right and wrong, what is beneficial and what is harmful. Therefore a theory must be judged by three tests. What are these three tests of a theory? Its origin, its validity, and its applicability. How do we judge its origin? We judge it by comparing the theory with the deeds of the sage kings of antiquity. How do we judge its validity? We judge it by comparing the theory with the evidence of the eyes and ears of the people. And how do we judge its applicability? We judge it by observing whether, when the theory is put into practice in the administration, it brings benefit to the state and the people. This is what is meant by the three tests of a theory.

Now among the gentlemen of the world there are those who believe in the existence of fate. Let us try examining this belief in the light of what we know of the sage kings. In ancient times chaos prevailed under Chieh, but T'ang followed him and there was order; chaos prevailed under Chou, but King Wu followed him and there was order. Within a single generation, with the same people, the world was in chaos under Chieh and Chou, and well ordered under T'ang and Wu. How then can we say that order or chaos in the world are decreed by fate? [1]

Yet there are still some gentlemen in the world who believe in the existence of fate. Let us try examining this belief in the light of the writings of the former kings. Among the writings of the former kings are those that were issued by the state and promulgated among the people, and these were called "stat-

[1] This argument, needless to say, does not refute the claims of the fatalists, who can just as well assert that the decree of fate changed abruptly when the rule passed from Chieh to T'ang and from Chou to Wu.

utes." Among the statutes of the former kings, were there ever any that said: "Good fortune cannot be sought for and bad fortune cannot be avoided. Being reverent will not help your chances, and doing evil will not harm them."? The writings by which law cases were settled and crimes punished were called "codes of punishment." Among the codes of punishment of the former kings, were there ever any that said: "Good fortune cannot be sought for and bad fortune cannot be avoided. Being reverent will not help your chances, and doing evil will not harm them."? The writings by which the armies were organized and the soldiers commanded to advance or retreat were called "declarations." Among the declarations of the former kings, were there ever any that said: "Good fortune cannot be sought for and bad fortune cannot be avoided. Being reverent will not help your chances, and doing evil will not harm them."? I have not exhausted all the evidence—it would be impossible to cite all the excellent writings in the world—but have enumerated only a few important examples, namely, the three types of writings mentioned above. Yet no matter how we search, we can find no evidence to support the theories of the fatalists. Should not such theories be rejected then?

To accept the theories of the fatalists would be to overthrow righteousness in the world. To overthrow righteousness in the world would be to replace it with the concept of fate and create worry for the people. And to expound a doctrine that creates worry for the people is to destroy the men of the world.

Why do we desire righteous men to be in authority? Because when righteous men are in authority, the world will be ordered, the Lord on High, the hills and rivers, and the ghosts and spirits will have worshipers to sacrifice to them, and the people will enjoy great benefit. How do we know? Mo Tzu said: In ancient times T'ang was enfeoffed in Po. Making allowances for the irregular boundary line, his domain measured only a hundred square *li*. He worked with his people for universal love and mutual benefit, and shared with them what was in abundance. He led his people to honor Heaven and serve the spirits above, and therefore Heaven and the spirits enriched him, the feudal lords became his allies, the people loved him, and worthy men came to serve him. Before he died he became ruler of the world and leader of the other lords.

In former times King Wen was enfeoffed in Chou at Mount Ch'i. Making allowances for the irregular boundary line, his domain measured only a hundred square *li*. He worked with his people for universal love and mutual benefit, and shared with them what was in abundance. So those nearby found security in his government and those far away were won by his virtue. All those who heard of King Wen rose up and went to him, and the morally weak, the unworthy, and the crippled who could not rise stayed where they were and pleaded, saying, "Couldn't the domain of King Wen be extended to our borders, so that we too could benefit? Why can't we too be like the people of King Wen?" Therefore Heaven and the spirits enriched him, the feudal lords became his allies, the people loved him, and worthy men came to serve him. Before he died he became ruler of the world and leader of the other lords. Previously I said that when righteous men are in authority, the world will be ordered, the Lord on High, the hills and rivers, and the ghosts and spirits will have worshipers to sacrifice to them, and the people will enjoy great benefit. And this is how I know that it is so.

Therefore the ancient sage kings issued statutes and published laws, providing rewards and punishments in order to encourage good and prevent evil. So men were loving and filial to their parents at home and respectful and friendly to the people of their neighborhood. Their actions showed a sense of propriety, their comings and goings a sense of restraint, and their relations with the opposite sex a sense of decorum. Thus, if they were put in charge of a government bureau, they did not steal or plunder; assigned to guard a city, they did not betray their trust or rebel. If their lord encountered difficulties, they would risk death for him; if he was forced to flee the state, they would accompany him into exile. Conduct like this was what the authorities rewarded and people praised. And yet the advocates of fatalism say: "Whoever is rewarded by the authorities was destined by fate to be rewarded. It is not because of his worthiness that he is rewarded!"

If this were so, then men would not be loving or filial to their parents at home nor respectful and friendly to the people of their neighborhood. Their actions would show no sense of propriety, their comings and goings no sense of restraint, and their relations with the opposite sex no sense of decorum. Put in charge of a government bureau, they would steal and plunder; assigned to guard a city, they would betray their trusts or rebel. If their lord encountered difficulty, they would not risk death for him; if he was forced to flee the state, they would not accompany him into exile. Conduct like this is what the authorities punish and the people condemn, and yet the advocates of fatalism say: "Whoever is punished by the authorities was destined by fate to be punished. It is not because of his evil actions that he is punished!" Believing this, rulers would not be righteous and subjects would not be loyal; fathers would not be loving and sons would not be filial; older brothers would not be brotherly and younger brothers would not be respectful. Those who insist upon holding such views are the source of pernicious doctrines. Theirs is the way of evil men!

How do we know that fatalism is the way of evil men? In ancient times there were impoverished people who were greedy for food and drink and lazy in pursuing their tasks, and as a result they did not have enough food and clothing, and found themselves troubled by cold and hunger. But they did not have sense enough to say, "We are weak in virtue and unworthy, and we have not been diligent in pursuing our tasks." Instead they said, "Fate has decreed that we shall be poor!" In ancient times there were evil kings who could not control the passions of their ears and eyes, or the wicked desires of their hearts. They did not follow the way of their ancestors, and so in time they lost their countries and brought destruction to their altars of the soil and grain. But they did not have sense enough to say, "We are weak in virtue and unworthy, and have not governed well." Instead they said, "Fate has decreed that we shall fail!"

The "Announcement of Chung Hui" says: "I have heard that the man of Hsia, pretending that he was acting under the mandate of Heaven, issued orders to his people. God was displeased and destroyed his hosts." [2] This shows how T'ang condemned Chieh's belief in fate. [3]

The "Great Declaration" says: "Chou lived in insolence and would not serve the Lord on High and the spirits. He cast

[2] The "man of Hsia" is Chieh; Chung Hui is identified as a minister of King T'ang, who overthrew Chieh. Both this and the following quotation are presumably from lost sections of the *Book of Documents*.

[3] Mo Tzu apparently feels justified in making this statement because the words translated as "mandate" and "orders" are written with the same character as the word "fate." Taken in context, however, the words are so far apart in meaning that the quotation can hardly be said to prove that Chieh believed in fate.

aside his ancestors and the spirits and would not sacrifice to them, saying, 'My people are ruled by fate.' He gave himself up to arrogance and tyranny, and Heaven thereupon cast him aside and would not protect him." This shows how King Wu condemned Chou's belief in fate.

Now if we were to accept the theories of the fatalists, then those above would not attend to affairs of state and those below would not pursue their tasks. If those above do not attend to affairs of state, then the government will fall into disorder, while if those below do not pursue their tasks, there will not be enough wealth and goods. There will be no way to provide millet and wine for offerings to the Lord on High and the spirits above, and no way to provide security for the worthy and able men of the world below. There will be no means to entertain and conduct exchanges with the feudal lords who come as guests from abroad, while within the state there will be no means to feed the hungry, clothe the cold, and care for the aged and weak. Hence fatalism brings no benefit to Heaven above, no benefit to the spirits in the middle realm, and no benefit to mankind below. Those who insist upon holding such views are the source of pernicious doctrines, and theirs is the way of evil men.

Therefore Mo Tzu said: If the gentlemen of the world truly hate poverty and wish to enrich the world, if they truly hate disorder and wish to bring order to the world, then they cannot but condemn the doctrines of the fatalists, for these bring great harm to the world.

AGAINST CONFUCIANS
PART I

(SECTION 39)

The Confucians[1] say: "There are degrees to be observed in treating relatives as relatives, and gradations to be observed in honoring the worthy."[2] They prescribe differences to be observed between close and distant relatives and between the honored and the humble. Their code of rites says: "Mourning for a father or mother should last three years; for a wife or eldest son, three years; for a paternal uncle, brother, or younger son, one year; and for other close relatives, five months." Now if the length of the mourning period is determined by the degree of kinship, then close relatives should be mourned for a long period and distant relatives for a short one. Yet the

---

[1] The word *ju*, translated here as "Confucians," denotes a group of scholars in Chou times who devoted particular attention to matters of ritual and etiquette. Confucius became their most renowned representative, and after his time the word customarily refers to his disciples and those scholars who followed his teachings. The *Huai-nan Tzu*, a work of the 2d century B.C., states (ch. 21) that Mo Tzu himself in his youth studied the teachings of the *ju*.

[2] The "Doctrine of the Mean," a section of the Confucian *Book of Rites*, contains a passage much like this. "Benevolence is acting like a human being, and the most important part of it is treating one's relatives as relatives. Righteousness is doing what is right, and the most important part of it is honoring the worthy. The degrees to be observed in treating one's relatives as relatives, and the gradations to be observed in honoring the worthy, are the result of ritual principles" (*Chung yung* XX, 5). Legge translates the phrase *ch'in ch'in* as "loving (one's) relatives," but I have used the more literal "treating one's relatives as relatives" in order to distinguish this type of love from the very different "universal love" advocated by Mo Tzu.

Confucians mourn the same length of time for a wife or eldest son as for a father or mother. And if the length of the mourning period is determined by the degree of honor due, then this means that the wife and eldest son are honored the same as the father and mother, while the paternal uncles and brothers are placed on the same level as younger sons! What could be more perverse than this? [3]

When a parent dies, the Confucians lay out the corpse for a long time before dressing it for burial while they climb up onto the roof, peer down the well, poke in the ratholes, and search in the washbasins, looking for the dead man. If they suppose that they will really find the dead man there, then they must be stupid indeed, while if they know that he is not there but still search for him, then they are guilty of the greatest hypocrisy. [4]

When a Confucian takes a wife, he goes to fetch her in person. Wearing a formal black robe, he acts as his own coachman, holding the reins and handing her the cord by which to pull herself up into the carriage, as though he were escorting an honored parent. The wedding ceremonies are conducted with as much solemnity as the sacrifices to the ancestors. High

---

[3] Mo Tzu is assuming that there is a closer relationship between a man and his parents than between a man and his wife and children, and that he owes greater respect to his parents and elder relatives than to his younger ones. The Confucians agreed in principle with these assumptions but, as we may see from their rules for mourning, modified them somewhat in practice.

[4] These were ancient practices handed down from the time when people really believed that they could find the soul of the dead man and bring him back to life. The Confucians, with their fondness for old rites, probably continued to practice them in Mo Tzu's time. Confucian works such as the *Book of Rites* actually advocate the practice of "ascending the roof" to call back the dead man, not because such rituals were believed to have any real efficacy, but because they were regarded as fitting expressions of love for the deceased.

and low are turned upside down, and parents are disregarded and scorned. Parents are brought down to the level of the wife, and the wife is exalted at the expense of service to the parents. How can such conduct be called filial? The Confucians say: "One takes a wife in order that she may aid in the sacrifices to the ancestors, and the son who is born of the union will in time become responsible for maintaining the ancestral temple. Therefore the wife and son are highly regarded." But we reply that this is false and misleading. A man's uncles and older brothers may maintain the temple of the ancestors for many years, and yet when they die the Confucian will mourn for them only one year. The wives of his brothers may aid in the sacrifices to the ancestors, and yet when they die he will not mourn for them at all. It is obvious, therefore, that the Confucians do not mourn three years for wives and eldest sons because wives and eldest sons maintain or aid in the sacrifices. Such concern for one's wife and son is a troublesome involvement, and in addition the Confucians try to pretend that it is for the sake of their parents. In order to favor those whom they feel the most partiality for, they slight those whom they should respect the most. Is this not the height of perversity?

In addition, the Confucians believe firmly in the existence of fate and propound their doctrine, saying, "Long life or early death, wealth or poverty, safety or danger, order or disorder are all decreed by the will of Heaven and cannot be modified. Failure and success, rewards and punishments, good fortune and bad are all fixed. Man's wisdom and strength can do nothing." If the various officials believe such ideas, they will be lax in their duties; and if the common people believe them, they will neglect their tasks. If the officials fail to govern properly, disorder will result; and if agriculture is neglected, poverty will result. Poverty and disorder destroy the basis of the government, and yet the Confucians accept such ideas, believing that they are the doctrine of the Way. Such men are the destroyers of the people of the world!

Moreover, the Confucians corrupt men with their elaborate and showy rites and music and deceive parents with lengthy mournings and hypocritical grief. They propound fatalism, ignore poverty, and behave with the greatest arrogance. They turn their backs on what is important, abandon their tasks, and find contentment in idleness and pride. They are greedy for food and drink and too lazy to work, but though they find themselves threatened by hunger and cold, they refuse to change their ways. They behave like beggars, stuff away food like hamsters, stare like he-goats, and walk around like castrated pigs. When superior men laugh at them, they reply angrily, "What do you fools know about good Confucians?" In spring and summer they beg for grain, and after the harvests have been gathered in they follow around after big funerals, with all their sons and grandsons tagging along. If they can get enough to eat and drink and get themselves put in complete charge of a few funerals, they are satisfied. What wealth they possess comes from other men's families, and what favors they enjoy are the products of other men's fields. When there is a death in a rich family, they are overwhelmed with joy, saying, "This is our chance for food and clothing!"

The Confucians say: "The superior man must use ancient speech and wear ancient dress before he can be considered benevolent." But we answer: The so-called ancient speech and dress were all modern once, and if at that time the men of antiquity used such speech and wore such dress, then they must not have been superior men. Must we then wear the dress of those who were not superior men and use their speech before we can be considered benevolent?

Again the Confucians say: "The superior man should be a follower and not a maker." [5] But we answer: In ancient times Yi invented the bow, Yü invented armor, Hsi-chung invented carts, and the craftsman Ch'iu invented boats. Do the Confucians mean, then, that the tanners, armorers, cart-makers and carpenters of today are all superior men and Yi, Yü, Hsi-chung, and the craftsman Ch'iu were all inferior men? Moreover, someone must have invented the ways which the Confucians follow, so that in following them they are, by their own definition, following the ways of inferior men.

The Confucians also say: "When the superior man is victorious in battle, he does not pursue the fleeing enemy. He protects himself with his armor, but does not shoot his arrows, and if his opponents turn and run, he will help them push their heavy carts." But we answer: If the contestants are all benevolent men, then they will have no cause to become enemies. Benevolent men instruct each other in the principles of giving and taking, right and wrong. Those without a cause will follow those who have a cause; those without wisdom will follow those who are wise. When they have no valid arguments of their own, they will submit to the arguments of others; when they see good, they will be won by it. How then could they become enemies? And if both parties in the struggle are evil, then although the victor does not pursue his fleeing opponents, protects himself with his armor but refrains from shooting them, and helps them push their heavy carts if

[5] Probably a reference to Confucius' description of himself as "a transmitter, and not a maker" (*Analects* VII, 1). The verb *tso*, "to make," may also mean "to invent."

they turn and run—though he does all these things, he will still never be considered a superior man. Let us suppose that a sage, in order to rid the world of harm, raises his troops and sets out to punish an evil and tyrannical state. But, having gained victory, he employs the methods of the Confucians and orders his soldiers, saying: "Do not pursue the fleeing enemy! Protect yourselves with your armor but do not shoot your arrows, and if your opponents turn and run, help them push their heavy carts." Then the evil and disorderly men will get away alive, and the world will not be rid of harm. This is to inflict cruelty upon the parents of the world and do the age a great injury. Nothing could be more unrighteous.

Again the Confucians say: "The superior man is like a bell. Strike it and it will sound; do not strike it and it will remain silent." But we answer: The superior man exerts the utmost loyalty in serving his lord and strives for filial piety in serving his parents. If those whom he serves achieve goodness, he will praise them; and if they have any fault, he will admonish them. This is the way of a subject. Now if one sounds only when struck and remains silent otherwise, then one will be concealing his knowledge and sparing his strength, waiting in dumb silence until he has been questioned. Though he may know of some way to bring benefit to his lord or parents, he will not mention it unless asked. A great revolt may be about to break out, bandits to rise up, or some trap to spring, and no one knows of it but himself, and yet, though he is actually in the presence of his lord or his parents, he will not mention it unless asked. This is the most perverse kind of treason! As subjects such men are disloyal; as sons they are unfilial. They are disrespectful in serving their elder brothers and unfaithful in their dealings with others.

Though one may prefer not to speak out in court before

being questioned, he should at least be concerned to speak out when he sees something that will profit himself. And if the ruler makes some proposal that does not seem beneficial, one should fold one's hands, gaze at the ground and, speaking in a hoarse voice as though lost in thought, reply, "I do not fully understand the matter. Though it is an emergency, we must avoid acting wrongly." [6]

Every doctrine, discipline, and standard of benevolence and righteousness is intended on a larger scale to be used in governing men, and on a smaller scale to fit one for holding office; abroad it is to be spread among all men, and at home it serves for self-cultivation. One should not abide in unrighteousness nor practice what is not in accordance with principle. He should work to promote what is beneficial to the world, both directly and indirectly, and avoid what is of no benefit. This is the way of the superior man. And yet, from what we have heard of the conduct of Confucius, it was exactly the opposite of this.

Duke Ching of Ch'i asked Master Yen,[7] "What sort of man is Confucius?" Master Yen did not reply. The duke asked once more, but again Master Yen did not reply. Duke Ching said, "Many people have spoken to me about Confucius, and all of them believed him to be a worthy man. Now when I ask you about him, why don't you answer?"

Master Yen replied, "I am a worthless person and incapable of recognizing a worthy man when I see one. But I have heard

[6] The translation of this paragraph is highly tentative.

[7] Master Yen or Yen Ying (d. 500 B.C.), acted as chief minister to Duke Ching and two of his predecessors. He was noted for his emphasis upon frugality in government and was a favorite figure of Mo-ist writers. A collection of anecdotes about Yen Ying and the rulers he served, strongly colored by Mo-ist thinking, is preserved under the title *Yen-tzu ch'un-ch'iu* (Spring and autumn of Master Yen).

it said that when a worthy man enters a foreign state, he will do his best to promote friendly relations between its ruler and its subjects and to dispel hatred between superiors and subordinates. Yet when Confucius went to the state of Ching, he knew that the lord of Po was plotting revolt, and yet he aided him by introducing Shih Ch'i to him. As a result the ruler almost lost his life and the lord of Po suffered punishment.[8] I have also heard that when a worthy man obtains favor with those above, he does not waste the opportunity, and when he obtains favor with those below, he does nothing dangerous. If his words are heeded by the ruler, they will bring benefit to men; if his doctrines are carried out by those below, they will bring benefit to the ruler. His words are plain and easy to understand; his conduct is plain and easy to follow. His conduct and righteousness enlighten the people; His plans and schemes bring understanding to the lord and his ministers. Now Confucius conceived deep plans and far-reaching schemes in the service of a traitor. He racked his brain and exhausted his wisdom in carrying out evil. To encourage subordinates to rebel against their superiors and teach subjects how to murder their lords is not the conduct of a worthy man! To enter a foreign state and ally oneself with its traitors is not the mark of a righteous man. To realize that men are being disloyal and yet urge them on to rebellion is not in accordance with benevolence and righteousness, To hide from others and then plot, to flee from others and then speak—this

---

[8] The lord of Po, a prince of the state of Ch'u (or Ching, as the text designates it here), led a revolt against the ruler of Ch'u in 479 B.C., the year of Confucius' death. He was quickly defeated and committed suicide. According to all reliable sources, both Duke Ching and Yen Ying had by this time been dead for some years. There is likewise no evidence that Confucius ever had any connection with the lord of Po or his famous retainer, Shih Ch'i.

is not the kind of conduct and righteousness that enlightens the people; this is not the kind of planning and scheming that brings understanding to the ruler and his ministers. I cannot see how Confucius is any different from the lord of Po. That is why I did not answer your question."

Duke Ching said, "I have benefited greatly by your works. If it were not for you, I would never have realized that Confucius is the same as the lord of Po!"

Confucius went to the state of Ch'i and had an interview with Duke Ching. Duke Ching was pleased with him and wanted to enfeoff him in Ni-ch'i. When he announced his intention to Master Yen, the latter said, "That will not do! The Confucians behave in an arrogant and self-righteous manner, which makes it impossible for them to set a good example for their subordinates. They love music and corrupt others, which makes it impossible to entrust them with a personal share in the government. They preach fatalism and neglect their tasks, which makes it impossible to entrust them with an office. They make much of funerals and seek to prolong grief, which makes it impossible for them to take proper care of the people. They wear strange clothes and affect a humble manner, which makes it impossible for them to be leaders of the multitude. Confucius, with his imposing appearance and attention to elaborate detail, misleads the age. With his music and dancing he attracts followers; with his multitude of ritual prescriptions to be observed in ascending and descending stairs he propounds his ceremonies; with his emphasis upon the rules for hastening and scurrying about court he impresses the multitude. His broad learning is of no use in deciding what is right for the age; his labored thinking does nothing to aid the people. One could live a couple of lifetimes and still not master all the learning of the Confucians;

in all those years one could not succeed in carrying out all their rites; while the largest fortune would not be sufficient to cover the expenses of their music. With their attention to appearance and detail and their evil practices they delude the rulers of the time; with their elaborate musical performances they corrupt the ignorant people. Their doctrines cannot be used as a model for the age; their learning cannot be used to guide the multitude. Now you intend to enfeoff Confucius because you hope he will reform the customs of the people of Ch'i, but this is not the way to lead the nation and guide the multitude!"

"Very well," said the duke. After that he treated Confucius with generosity and courtesy but withheld the fief. He received him with respect but did not inquire about his doctrines.

Confucius was furious and grew angry at Duke Ching and Master Yen. He persuaded Ch'ih-i Tzu-p'i to become a follower of T'ien Ch'ang and then, having told Master Hui of Nan-kuo what he wanted done, returned to Lu.[9] After a while, word came that Ch'i was planning to attack Lu. Confucius said to his disciple Tzu-kung, "Tz'u, now is the time to begin the great undertaking!" He then sent Tzu-kung to Ch'i, where, through the introduction of Master Hui of Nan-kuo,

[9] The T'iens, who had originally been rulers of the state of Ch'en and are therefore often referred to by the surname Ch'en, were a powerful ministerial family of Ch'i who eventually overthrew the ducal house of Ch'i and assumed rulership of the state. In 481 B.C., two years before Confucius died, T'ien Ch'ang assassinated Duke Chien of Ch'i, and this is the "revolt" referred to later on. As in the previous anecdote, the Mo-ists are attempting to show that Confucius and his disciples were at the bottom of all this dirty work, though there is no evidence in other sources to support this. On the contrary, *Analects* XIV, 22, and *Tso chuan*, Duke Ai 14, tell us that, when T'ien Ch'ang assassinated Duke Chien, Confucius personally urged the duke of Lu to undertake an expedition to punish him.

he was able to see T'ien Ch'ang. He urged T'ien Ch'ang to attack Wu instead of Lu, and persuaded Kao-kuo Pao-yen not to interfere with T'ien Ch'ang's plans for revolt. Then he went and urged Yüeh to attack Wu. For three years both Ch'i and Wu were in danger of being destroyed, and the corpses of the dead piled up in countless numbers. This was due to the scheming of Confucius.

When Confucius was acting as minister of justice in Lu, he spurned the ducal house and supported Chi Sun.[10] Chi Sun was prime minister of Lu, but he ran away from his post and, as he was struggling with the men of the city to get out the gate, Confucius lifted up the gate bar for him.

Once, when Confucius was in trouble between Ts'ai and Ch'en, he lived for ten days on soups made of greens without any rice mixed in.[11] His disciple Tzu-lu boiled a pig for him, and Confucius ate the meat without asking where it had come from. Tzu-lu also robbed someone of his robe and exchanged it for wine, and Confucius drank the wine without asking where it came from. But when he was received by Duke Ai of Lu, Confucius refused to sit down unless his mat was straight, and refused to eat unless the food was cut up properly. Tzu-lu came forward and asked, "Why do you do the opposite of what you did when we were between Ch'en and Ts'ai?"

Confucius said, "Come here, and I will tell you. At that time we were intent upon staying alive. Now we are intent

[10] Chi Sun was a member of a powerful ministerial family of Lu that, like the T'ien family in Ch'i, had in effect usurped control of the government from the ducal family. Again there is no evidence to support the charges made against Confucius.

[11] The fact that Confucius and his disciples, in the course of their travels, ran out of provisions in the area of the states of Ch'en and Ts'ai, is attested by *Analects* XV. The rest of the anecdote is apocryphal.

upon acting righteously." Thus when Confucius was starving and in trouble, he did not hesitate to grab at anything at all to keep himself alive, but when he was satiated he behaved hypocritically in order to appear refined. What greater vileness and hypocrisy could there be?

Once, while Confucius was sitting and chatting with his disciples, he said, "When Shun saw Ku Sou, he felt uneasy. At that time, the empire was in danger.[12] Tan, the duke of Chou, was not a benevolent man, was he? Why did he abandon his home and go off to live alone?" [13]

Such was the conduct of Confucius and the way his mind worked. His followers and disciples all imitated him. Thus, Tzu-kung and Chi Lu aided K'ung Li in raising a revolt in the state of Wei; Yang Huo revolted in Ch'i; Pi Hsi held the territory of Chung-mou in rebellion; and Ch'i Tiao suffered a mutilating punishment. No one could be worse than these men! [14]

Disciples and students, following their teacher, will practice

[12] Ku Sou was the evil father of Shun. The remark is found in many early works, and is customarily interpreted to mean that Shun was uneasy at the thought that, though ruler of the empire, he was obliged to remain respectful and obedient to such an evil parent. The Mo-ists, however, apparently interpreted it as an attack by Confucius on the character of Shun. There is no evidence that Confucius actually made the remark.

[13] A legend, repeated elsewhere in the *Mo Tzu* (ch. 11, sec. 46), says that the duke of Chou, brother of King Wu, resigned from his ministerial position at court and retired for a time to his fief in Lu. Since he was revered as a sage, the Mo-ists are attempting to damage Confucius' reputation by picturing him as sneering at the duke of Chou.

[14] Tzu-kung and Chi Lu, i.e., Tzu-lu, were disciples of Confucius. There is no evidence, however, that the former had anything to do with the revolt in Wei, and the name should perhaps be emended to Tzu-kao, an official of Wei who was said to have been a disciple of Confucius. Tzu-lu's part in the revolt, which took place in 480 B.C., is recorded in *Tso chuan*, Duke Ai 15. The other men mentioned seem to have had little or no connection with Confucius.

his doctrines and use his conduct as a model, only in some cases their strength and wisdom are not equal to those of the teacher. Now if Confucius behaved in such a way, it is obvious that Confucian scholars should be regarded with suspicion!

INDEX